The Theory of Spiritual Human Behavior

The Color of Psychology: Spirituality, Human Behavior, and Purpose

ISBN: 978-1-944901-38-7

Copyright © 2025 by Speaking Freedom LLC
All rights reserved.
No portion of this book may be reproduced without written permission from the publisher or author, except as permitted by U.S. copyright law.

Holy Bible, New International Version®, NIV® Copyright ©1973, 1978, 1984, 2011 by Biblica, Inc.® Used by permission. All rights reserved worldwide.

Unless otherwise indicated, all Scripture quotations are taken from THE MESSAGE, copyright © 1993, 2002, 2018 by Eugene H. Peterson. Used by permission of NavPress. All rights reserved. Represented by Tyndale House Publishers, Inc.

Book Cover by: Kaci Winslow

Publisher Website: speakingfreedom.org

Other Website Information: SpeakingfreedomTV.org, edu-freedom.org

Publisher Address: 75 Washington St. #1177, Fairburn, GA 30213

Speaking Freedom Books Disclaimers

We appreciate your purchase and look forward to helping you grow in all areas of your life.

We hope you find all the necessary information for your growth. God bless.

If you are currently under a physician's care, please maintain that relationship. This audiobook is not intended to stop your current treatment plan. If you require medical attention, please consult a qualified healthcare professional.

Please note: All results are based on the individual's ability to adapt and adjust to an environment or situation. We are not responsible for the results you achieve. The life-enhancement coaches at Speaking Freedom provide information to help you grow.

You are responsible for maintaining that growth, taking on and applying the information to your individual life as needed.

This book was written by Speaking Freedom Books.

Concept by: Kaci (Winslow) Myers

Speaking Freedom Books   Spiritual Human Behavior

For optimal results, you will need an open mind, the ability to conduct thorough research, and a balanced approach to your lifestyle.

Spiritual Human Behavior
Introduction

The concept of Spiritual Human Behavior aims to explain how the soul's growth, development, and activity influence the behavior of all individuals on Earth. It also explores how life impacts the soul and how the soul illuminates one's purpose. Developing your soul involves learning to process emotions related to your life experiences and reframing the narrative of your story in your mind. Over time, the methods adapted from this theory help to Align your maturity level with your age through a shift in your mindset.

The discovery of this theory stemmed from observing and evaluating how people develop based on their ability to embrace their lives and struggles, allowing them to mature internally, as opposed to those who do not confront their issues. Individuals with classic avoidance tendencies tend to avoid addressing their daily concerns or past experiences, which now shape who they are today. Many people invest a considerable amount of time attempting to change their outer appearance, often fleeing from their true selves, while inside, they have yet to tackle the issues that contribute to their feelings of inferiority.

The Concept includes understanding the steps that follow forgiveness. You forgive the other person and forget the offense, hopefully learning a valuable lesson. From there, you must work on forgiving them, allowing them to be released, and healing yourself. This process enables you to be free from the anxiety of what happened, freeing you from the fear that it will happen again and releasing you from the burden of holding onto it, which can contribute to developing various illnesses.

The Theory of Spiritual Human Behavior aims to help you understand your spiritual growth and its contribution to becoming a better person. It also helps address the issues that have impacted you and those that trigger emotional responses, ultimately seeking to control your life.

Speaking Freedom's series of books about faith, spirituality, and overcoming adversity shows how we arrived at the overall theory of spiritual human behavior.

Overview

To Understand spiritual human behavior is to understand yourself. It'll help you understand your interests, choices, decision-making process, and problem-solving approach. It will also help you understand yourself better and cultivate self-love, embracing yourself as you accept the differences of others, recognizing that we are all raised differently and come from different environmental backgrounds, heritages, and belief systems.

Considering those baseline factors makes it easier to look at our neighbors, brothers, sisters, and the people around us and accept them for who they are, just as we wish to be accepted for who we are. This understanding comes with the recognition that each person develops, grows, and becomes whom they are meant to be unique. The reason for these differences lies in our individual conversations with God.

Soul Assignment

When we have this individual conversation with God, we are given a list of things we can do here on Earth with options. The process resembles the game of life in which you select the path you will follow. Speaking Freedom believes that, before arriving on Earth, each soul, through the power of free will, chooses the course it will undertake and the challenges it will face.

Please note that every decision you make on this journey is like navigating a constantly shifting maze. Regardless of what you say or do, your daily decisions significantly impact other aspects of your life. If you create a dream board, vision board, or goal list, these lists and boards can alter the path you envision and the experiences you have in your life.

Life experiences do not negate the journey of the soul. Every person faces specific challenges throughout their lifetime. One's life's calling will often be evident in negative and positive situations. For example, those called to be leaders will find their souls guiding them to lead in any environment, and their upbringing will influence how, where, and when this guidance occurs.

Of course, how a person handles it, which method they choose to circumvent, pursue, or overcome it, will determine where their soul grows, where it is stunted, and how they will progress. Additionally, we all have different life paths. We all have specific journeys that we are designed to take here on Earth.

Within those journeys, you'll face different trials and tribulations and the things you must grow from to become the best version of yourself. The thing is, we're not all protected as children. We're not all given a perfect life where everything is handed to us, or certain things always go our way.

Most people are not born into wealth, nor is everyone gifted with untapped talent. Recognizing that we each have unique life paths, we are responsible for embracing, accepting, and nurturing our personal development through our experiences.

Spiritual human behavior aids individuals in addressing unresolved issues within themselves, even after they have healed, forgiven, and let go. Despite overcoming challenges, there are still aspects of life where we must offer ongoing support to one another, demonstrating that we have faced similar struggles and illustrating how such experiences contribute to the growth of our souls.

Speaking Freedom offers ways to nurture your soul by integrating your actions, thoughts, and the evolution of your spirit as you confront the challenges that arise and learn valuable lessons from your trials, tribulations, and mistakes. As you grow, the results you didn't like turn into those you're in love with and create the life you want for the rest of your life.

This theory works by shaking every loose thing within you, allowing you to understand and embrace yourself, understand others more clearly, and appreciate each person's unique level of life, living, and understanding. All preliminary information can be used with The Non-Religious Guide to Faith series.

Spiritual human behavior is a psychological theory that encompasses but is not limited to, the belief in God and oneself, self-love, and addressing any aspect of life that affects you today. Given the understanding that some things may lie dormant after you've forgiven or forgotten the incident until triggered, we learn that we have not internally healed and released ourselves in a way that allows us to grow from the incident we faced.

*Please note: an incident does not have to be a traumatic experience or an experience that would have altered you physically.

These are matters you might avoid due to drinking, smoking, classic avoidance, and a reluctance to confront issues at all. The goal is to help you nurture your soul by addressing daily challenges. Your soul's growth and maturity do not depend on your age but rather on how you handle the obstacles you encounter and how you progress and learn from each experience, ensuring you don't repeatedly make the same mistakes or achieve the same outcomes due to unaddressed issues. When you truly understand who you are, you can overcome anything that comes your way. Anything you face can be conquered, and you will not feel like you are losing or missing out.

Although this is not a religious book, some portions of the Bible will be included in this particular book.

The part we're speaking of now is that God knew you before you were placed in your mother's belly. So if God knew you, he sent you here with a course and a purpose that you are to carry out, but that course and purpose must be awakened within you. Spiritual Human Behavior will explain how to determine and develop each area. Each person can be at different levels, but they all need to grow from one of these experiences.

Establishing The Journey

This portion of the overview establishes a basic understanding of the course and journey of the soul here on earth before we break down the mind/ spiritual nature, body/ vehicle, and heart/ soul.

Based on what we've already discussed about God knowing us before we were formed in our mothers' wombs, this leads us to understand that before we came to earth, there was already a predestined route and journey we would take during our time here. Throughout this journey, we have the freedom to make our own decisions. However, every time we make a choice that aligns us more closely with our purpose for coming to earth, it awakens our souls even more to our oneness with God.

Soul Purpose

Suppose the purpose of souls coming to Earth is to remember that they are angelic souls who chose to have a human experience. What does that mean to you?

This theory will assist you in awakening to your humanity and embracing an experience on Earth that is uniquely yours rather than imposed by someone else. The most remarkable aspect of your soul is that it resides within your heart and houses your true purpose.

However, your soul must be connected to your mind and spirit to awaken that purpose and enable your body to carry it out. We're addressing the mind, body, and soul. Remember, your mind encompasses your spirit. Your entire existence resides within the heart as the soul; your heart holds your purpose. Your body contains everything as a vessel. This is the trinity that we possess inside each of us.

Everyone has a purpose when they come to this earth. In this book, you will encounter various things and situations influenced by your upbringing. When you follow that path, each situation can teach you something and open yourself up to new experiences. This varies depending on how protective your parents were and what you were allowed to experience.

Each situation serves as a developmental point for you as an adult. The goal of spiritual human behavior is to ensure that adults are walking around in physical form. At the same time, internally, their undeveloped soul leads them to behave, think, and achieve results not of "Child-Like" faith but of an immature soul. There is a distinction between the developmental stages of a soul.

The different stages of soul development should correspond to your age and can be observed in behavior patterns and thought processes. Knowing this can help you identify areas where your soul is not in alignment, allowing you to begin developing it in ways that change your behavior.

The more you develop your soul, the more your mind changes. The more your mind aligns with your soul rather than what is presented to you, the more you develop as a person. This allows you to conquer challenges better, manifest your desires more effectively, and experience fulfillment, both in feeling fulfilled and helping others without manipulation, lies, cheating, or any other deceit. The Theory of Spiritual Human Behavior aims to transform how we think, approach situations, and confront challenges anew so that we can grow spiritually and physically, grounded in our souls' purpose.

As we begin to understand our path and the journey we are meant to take in this life, we can avoid basing our actions on others or their opinions, which do not align with the purpose of living our lives and do not yield the results we seek. Often, this stems from an imbalance due to unresolved issues we faced as children, challenges that affected us as young adults, or struggles we encounter today. Subsequently, we tend to mask these feelings through partying, work, social outings, and even church activities.

We must become individuals who can confront the challenges we face directly without minimizing them or resorting to addiction or escapism. We cannot continue attributing our issues to God while wondering why we struggle to find solutions or why the same problems persist. Nothing will change if we defer responsibility to God, the universal creator, expecting instant resolutions without putting in some work. This approach is unrealistic for the soul's growth.

The soul can have a harder time growing, being whole, and prospering if we do not seize the opportunity to address the challenges we face, take responsibility, and be accountable for both our good and bad choices- our positive decisions and those we view as mistakes as well as those we consider divinely purposed by God.

We must understand who we are, why we are, and where we are to nurture our souls and connect more deeply with God. This will manifest our desires and allow us to live the life we choose rather than the one we've been given. When we cultivate the ability to shed the victim mentality, we can become courageous and rise above challenges by learning the steps and patterns that lead to our continued success.

No successful millionaire winged it each day. They establish steps and practices. The goal is to develop methods for making informed decisions and consistently achieving the desired results.

This process helps you uncover your path to success, life cycles, journey, and purpose while learning to overcome challenges as they arise. We often overlook that the course and the journey unfold gradually, day by day. If we choose to fail at the same things as the day before, we are not contributing to our growth. We remain stagnant but can radiate vibrant energy externally if we grow internally.

We become vibrant inside by developing our souls by examining everything that affects our mentality. It doesn't matter what you consider; the people you date are influenced by those you were raised around, and what you accept in a relationship is shaped by what you were taught was acceptable unless you are mature enough to form your own beliefs based on your own experiences and research. If you do not recognize the factors that influence who you are daily, you're likely living a life guided by someone else's projections and not your desires.

It is okay to learn from others; however, abandoning your path for someone else's is unacceptable just because they didn't follow through on their own or don't want you to live your life and pursue your own journey.

We all have separate courses and unique DNA; although they connect, we remain distinct. Think about twins. They are not the same unless they are physically joined and require surgical separation. When you consider Siamese twins, who share a physical connection, they are still two individuals linked only by their bodies. I'm not sure if such cases are commonly observed today since there are numerous preventative measures in place to terminate a pregnancy when such situations arise.

Understanding The Soul

Your soul resides in the depths of your heart, and you perceive the world around you with your soul. That's why you must guard your heart. Your heart can be heartened or strengthened, and your innocence is found within it.

Your heart is where your innocence is found and the core of who you are. Your mind and spirit receive from your heart and soul. As you self-evaluate, you become intrigued by the possibilities of being your best self. Running from your problems will cause you to regress instead of progressing into your highest self. Your soul must be awakened for your mind to receive spiritual updates as you mature. Your mind needs to understand that there is more to you than what you show on the surface and how you've learned to survive.

Spiritual Human Behavior aims to help you understand soul growth, purpose, and maturing with your soul as you age. The next thing you should know is that your actions display the state and development of your spiritual level. So there are spiritual babies, children, teenagers, young adults, mature and old souls.

Your actions are more likely to determine your soul level and growth than your words. You have to be able to account for and understand how your actions affect or are affected by your soul's growth.

A mature soul will not engage in what excites an immature soul. This may include random sexual partners, light drugs, hardcore drugs, or any other distractions, as spiritual human behavior is individualized and relies on each person's unique journey. I cannot dictate your actions, but they should reflect a greater maturity than a child's. Temper tantrums and breakdowns should not occur. It's OK to have something go on and be able to process and deal with it. But how you respond and act will tell how developed your soul is.

Spiritual Nature

Your mind encompasses your spiritual nature, while your heart encompasses your soul. Your soul is the core of your being, and your heart and soul nurture your growth from all that is within you.

This comes from the spiritual nature in which your brain encompasses your spiritual mind. Your whole body is the sperm that grew from within the womb, and your soul is what allows your mind to be fed.

If you feed your soul, mind, spiritual nature, and your body corresponds. Spiritual human behavior expounds on those various aspects: your spiritual mind, your heart, soul, and your body vessel because your body is just a tool that moves around. Your soul can operate and correspond with other people on any level.

Spiritual Human Behavior helps you radiate oneness with the Creator. This theory developed during my bachelor's degree in applied management, focusing on psychology. I started evaluating the people around me based on their personality traits and characteristics. That sorting process exposed me to various personality types and aspects I noticed within each type, including their zodiac signs, the environments they were raised in, their parental influences, and all these diverse factors that contribute to a person's character and spiritual human behavior.

I didn't refer to it as spiritual human behavior at that time. I was sorting through the various reasons behind people's actions and how they became who they are. This led me to group people by their similarities and the traits they exhibited.

It also proved helpful later when I made space for prayer and meditation. After studying all these concepts, I evaluated the maturity levels of individuals, which I later identified as soul maturity. I considered how their zodiac sign applied to them. Shortly after that, I learned from watching the Dr. Drew show that addiction, a form of out-of-control avoidance, prevents a person from maturing with age.

When I say addiction is a form of avoidance that is out of control, I mean that anything can be addictive behavior. Overindulging in church services and activities can become an addiction. Shopping can also be an addiction.

Working can be an addiction. Drugs can be an addiction. Alcohol can be an addiction.

Avoidance itself can be an addiction. Sex can be an addiction. Anything that has an unhealthy hold on you that you cannot control but that controls you and causes you to lie, steal, cheat, or engage in any behavior that can hurt the people you love constitutes an unhealthy addiction.

Figure out what you avoid thinking about or being a part of. What are you avoiding doing? What are you avoiding within yourself when you overindulge in these things?

During personal life transitions, I began developing theories that categorize most people's actions and patterns. After each theory was documented, thorough observations were conducted, and theories were presented in a beta-testing format. I started applying the theories to people's lives and making recommendations through social media. This process consistently results in positive outcomes, including identification, pathways to address issues, and individualized solutions, as each theory is applied to help overcome life's struggles.

Thinking Patterns

During the beta-testing period, new thinking patterns emerged, enabling clients to work through childhood issues that fostered their spiritual awareness, awaken their soul purpose, and apply and practice spiritual human behavior. Beyond the online beta testing and explanations of various theories, in-person, face-to-face clients benefited from meditating, praying, and utilizing the laws of attraction with the vision board, faith-based goals, and theories to manifest results.

During the evaluation process for entrance into the program, thorough research and an interview take place. During the interview, the life enhancement coaching specialists invest time to learn about the client and inquire about their hopes and dreams, fears, and belief limitations.

The evaluations aren't for the staff but for the aspects of self-serving information used by clients to develop new thinking patterns for each client. Determining the soul age is done on a very individual level, usually resulting from your actions, abilities, and the degree of love you have for yourself and others.

Mindset

Where you are physically can affect the development of your spirit and soul, changing the parameters of your mind.

Growth occurs in stages. Our other books on faith will help you understand, grow, and deepen your faith. Nurturing your faith is as essential as nurturing your soul; they go hand in hand.

To take steps toward your soul's purpose, you must have faith. Faith isn't a magical wand or anything like that. It is simply the belief in what you are doing to the extent that nothing can stop you from pursuing it.

Not because someone told you to, but because you genuinely believe in it for yourself, not based on anything else.

Spirituality Without Religion
How All Things Work Together

Spiritual Human Behavior differs from religious knowledge. Your soul's growth isn't determined by your familiarity with the Bible or your ability to speak eloquently.

Wisdom is based on how you apply what you know. Your soul's growth depends on how you use that knowledge, regardless of whether it's religious in nature. Any information you acquire- whether from experiences, individual interactions, or educational settings- should lead to some form of action; otherwise, you may know a lot, but it's a waste of information.

Please note that spiritual human behavior is not merely about knowing scriptures, reciting numerous Quran verses, or frequently attending church. It does not pertain to the mere accumulation of knowledge based on religious principles. Spiritual human behavior can be understood through each individual's personal growth, as depicted in the stories of the Bible.

For example, Jesus developed spiritually from every incident and situation he faced during his ministry and what he learned as a child. He could develop and grow in those situations by being open to God's knowledge. The more he grew, the more he changed the spiritual nature of his human behavior.

When you think about Paul, the more he grew, changed, and learned, the more he developed. When you consider Peter, the more he knew and could change, the better he became at what he could do.

When you think about Judas, he didn't know enough to do better with what he had learned. He was knowledgeable but lacked awareness of how to apply that knowledge or what he should have known. Therefore, he couldn't act on his insights. It's possible to know something yet not be aware of how to use it effectively, which hinders action. However, having that awareness and evaluating your life fosters personal growth and forgiveness of self.

You will learn more about The Judas Theory further in the content of the book.

Your knowledge does not determine how spiritual human behavior works in your life, and it's not based on your age. Just because you grow in age and years here does not mean you mature.

Maturity is part of the development of spiritual human behavior. Spiritual human behavior captures not only the high end but the entirety of the spectrum, whether you are advancing, stagnant, or growing into who you are meant to become. This theory will help break down the differences among these states and how they relate to you. It will also guide you on revisiting these aspects or gaining a new perspective, allowing you to assess and navigate your choices to make better decisions.

Non-Traditional Approach

Spiritual human behavior is not based on traditions learned or passed down. It's not founded on actions taken simply because they are traditional. You cannot apply tradition to it, as your journey may differ from that of others. If your journey makes someone else uncomfortable, tradition may have prevented them from achieving their highest purpose, reaching their goals, and gaining the knowledge essential for their value system, self-worth, and understanding the difference between acting because it's part of their journey and being slowed down by tradition.

Spiritual human behavior focuses on liberating you, shedding the burdens of others' expectations so you can connect with your needs and pursue your purpose and journey in this world. Religious thinking can hinder your experience as a human and the growth of the spiritual nature of human behavior.

You must also understand that spiritual human behavior stems from self-knowledge, self-love, and self-worth. You must recognize and accept yourself, including the good and the bad, as well as the things you can control and those you cannot.

You need to recognize the topics you prefer to avoid discussing. It is essential to identify these aspects and embrace, understand, and accept everything about yourself that you can control. Otherwise, you might not revisit and resolve specific situations. Some people may have done things to you, or you may have acted in ways that affected them. You can only forgive yourself and allow that forgiveness to heal you. This means that by forgiving yourself, you also forgive them.

Reflect on the issues you forgave to ensure you don't just try to forget them or act as if they didn't happen; instead, address those matters so that when you encounter something similar in the future, you'll know how to handle it. This understanding forms the foundation of our exploration into spiritual human behavior. This type of soul development impacts your growth, maturity level, and actions. Therefore, spiritual human behavior involves comprehending the reasons behind your challenges and how to embrace them for your personal growth.

You need to take everything you've experienced- good, bad, or indifferent- and reflect on it by asking, how can I grow from this information? What did I miss here that I can get right next time? If this same situation were to happen again, what would I do differently to change the outcome? Because nine times out of ten, you will face something similar.

Embracing your challenges, understanding them, and growing from all you know, experience, and connect with are all essential for developing spiritual human behavior, which focuses on addressing problems.

You cannot run from or avoid problems that significantly affect your ability to develop your soul and weaken your spiritual nature. Your spiritual nature reflects your mindset. How do you handle situations? What does your mindset receive from your soul and your knowledge, and how does your body enact those insights?

Numerology

In addition, knowing your life course will help you make better decisions and know your life number based on your date of birth. If you add all the numbers together and break it down to the lowest common number or the lowest number that you can come up with, so 1 - 10, 10 being 1, 11 being 2, 12 being 3, 13 being 4, 14 being 5, 15 being 6, 16 being 7, 17 being 8, 18 being 9 and 19 being 1 again. When you get to 1 again, you also need to know that all numbers added to 9 equal whatever number added to it.

So 9 plus 3 is 12, but it's 3. 9 plus 9 is 18, but it's 9 if you combine the numbers.

Learning your life number will help you understand portions of your life. If you are taking the course, you should already have your life cycle number handy.

If you are not taking one of the courses and you bought this book as a single purchase, calculate your life cycle number by adding your date of birth, your day, your month, and your year, and then whatever number that is, adding those two numbers together and making one single number. From there, websites so that you can discover some more about yourself. You may be able to track and cycle different areas of your life with your numerology number.

You can also get a paid-for report about your life cycle. It'll break down things you may experience and go through in different months. Personally, that was foundational because it allowed me to see and know if I could trust what I was learning enough to share it with you. I could say certain things happen around this time, and around that time, these things happen, and it would all coincide with what the reports said.

The real focus is what you must do within, with, or without the reports. You should look back over your life and see what you usually go through in January. We're not talking about taxes, returns, or anything like that. But what do you usually experience during this time? What do you typically experience during that time? Each month, try to figure out when your high months are, when your marginal months are, and when your lower months are.

These tools can assist you and help you understand your life more. They can help you combat/manage stress responses, organize your view of life, and set precedence for your purpose.

This is not based on somebody telling you something about your life; you start to consider when good things happen to you.

Every time something good happens for you, note what time of year it happens, what day it happens, and how it happened. Note as many things as possible that you find happening in cycles, maybe familiar, or something that you believe is notable and should be noted so that you can figure out when your good months are as well as your not-so-good months.

It can also be beneficial to consider your zodiac sign. Zodiac signs do not define who you are, but knowing that everyone born under a particular sign experiences both positives and negatives can be enlightening. Understanding the negatives is not meant for self-condemnation, to promote feelings of guilt, or to foster depression, as these experiences are common for those born during this time of year.

You learn the good, so you can continue to embrace those positive aspects. However, you also learn the not-so-good to recognize anything that may negatively affect your life. This awareness allows you to address those issues and achieve a more positive outcome, and it helps you better understand what you are facing.

Zodiac Signs

When dealing with zodiac signs, there are a lot of different things that affect who the person is. The zodiac sign serves as a baseline for the characteristics of each individual born under that sign. However, your maturity level will influence how you express those characteristics, and your maturity can be divided into several areas.

Someone may be mature in finances yet immature in relationships. A person might be mature in relationships yet struggle in business. Another individual could excel in relationships, finances, and business but face significant communication challenges. Someone else may communicate effectively and manage everything well yet fail to follow through or accomplish tasks.

The theory of spiritual human behavior involves learning about yourself, becoming more aware of who you are, and functioning better in life. Your mind holds your spiritual nature and memories, encompassing all that makes you who you are. Your soul carries your purpose and is the essence of everything, so you should safeguard it.

You should protect your heart and ensure that you are selective about what and who gets into it. Never let failure or success get to your heart or your head, but you need to make sure that you know as many things as possible that pertain to you on a spiritual, financial, and any other level that may be necessary.

It is essential to learn about your zodiac and understand how your maturity level influences it. Your environment can also have an effect; depending on how and where you grow up and who your influences are, you may or may not develop certain habits or learn from being raised around specific people.

If you were created to be a certain way, the environment in which you're raised could steer you in the opposite direction if it doesn't nurture your growth appropriately. There's no guarantee that you will turn out poorly based on the people around you, but part of this theory illustrates that you will either mirror what you experienced growing up or become its polar opposite. It's perfectly fine to be the opposite and equally acceptable to be the same.

The objective is for you to be as productive as possible as an adult, regardless of environmental factors. Once you learn these concepts, certain aspects of life may become clearer. The more things make sense, the better you will navigate the ongoing challenges based on your circumstances and identity in your surroundings. Your position or growth area can be spiritual, financial, educational, economic, mental, or any area you can identify with.

Life's Cycles

During this process, your developmental changes will change how you respond to your life cycle. So the things that you may have found yourself continuing to do over and over and over again with this type of growth, with this type of understanding and knowledge, you will be able to see yourself progress year after year, aligned with the same purpose, aligned with the same goals, but growing within your soul, which is allowing you to respond differently, which is allowing you to have different interests, different desires, both spiritually and physically. Now, there are many things you can begin to see changing.

It's similar to creating a vision board. As you work on this vision board, you slowly begin to see changes in your life.

As you grow, you will observe and learn about your life cycles. You will notice when things are going well, when they are upbeat, and when they are unfavorable.

You can improve any undesirable aspect and work on developing the areas where you're weaker. Rather than focusing solely on your weaknesses, acknowledge and grow within them while understanding how they affect you. Remember, each year on Earth is considered a complete life cycle. You calculate it from your date of birth and the time of conception, examining how the months you spent growing up correlate with your progress from year to year.

Once you calculate your life cycle, you may be able to identify different aspects of that nine-month cycle. In the next three months, you might discover specific patterns illuminating how spiritual human behavior indicates that a person can remain in a job, church, neighborhood, school, or community for an extended period without experiencing real progression, growth, or meaningful change.

Spiritual human behavior helps us identify and refine what keeps us trapped in cycles, generational curses, or any environment where we should be growing but are not experiencing change.

If you're not actively progressing in any direction or are more stagnant, you're comfortable wherever you are. Many factors must be considered in spiritual human behavior. If you're a medical professional, reflect on how "Spiritual Human Behavior" can be used within your practice or as a resource. Feel free to reach out.

If your question is, " How do you grow from understanding spiritual human behavior? " As a medical professional, you can help individuals recognize why their actions may not align with their stated intentions. You can assist them in understanding this concept through exposure therapy, though it is not the only method to employ. Each person is uniquely designed to respond differently to various approaches.

Hereditary Background & History

Spiritual human behavior involves understanding one's background, including where one comes from, environmental influences, and the impact of parental or guardian figures. It also encompasses recognizing one's personality traits and blood type. Evaluating and understanding oneself becomes essential to fostering individual growth if these factors shape who one is, how one behaves, and why one behaves that way.

It's important to note that some patterns are generational and harder to overcome, even when faced regularly. However, once you create new patterns, you can change the course of generational evolution. Suppose your family has always dealt with this in a certain way. In that case, it often returns to tradition rather than breaking away from what has historically been done, continuing the same ineffective methods passed down through generations.

Spiritual human behavior encourages you to examine the situation and reflect, "This is how it may have been handled in the past, and this is the outcome that resulted from that approach." But you seek a different outcome now. Therefore, to achieve a different result, you must alter your approach.

When applying this to yourself, you should assess every situation you encounter, and if you dislike the result obtained from the method, take time to evaluate your previous actions for recalibration.

Then, you will take the necessary steps to change those things until you achieve the desired results. The situation may not be the same next time, but it could be entirely the opposite. You are applying the principle to attempt to change what you believe you have done wrong.

If you feel you have made a mistake, that mistake serves as a lesson. What spiritual human behavior helps you evaluate your life, particularly in areas where you need to grow? If this is an area where I need to improve, what aspects must I address? These aspects may indeed be challenging to confront.

Spiritual human behavior can be pretty challenging when integrated into your life, and a common side effect is feeling overwhelmed.

You might encounter significant difficulties and prefer not to think about them afterward. However, it's essential to confront these issues. Spiritual human behavior involves addressing challenges because ignoring them can hinder spiritual growth and stunt maturity. Your soul needs to grow, develop, and mature to apply lessons to life, ensuring that later on, you do not continue to face the same dilemmas and receive the same results. Therefore, whatever you choose to do matters.

Reshaping Your Future

If you tied your shoe and didn't like how the laces were, you would go back through them and see which lace was incorrect. Whether twisted the wrong way or laced in the wrong space while rushing. If that's the case, you have to return to where you made the mistake and figure out what to do to fix it. This may not mean returning to a past relationship to understand what went wrong. Instead, it might mean that you're facing a similar situation in your current relationship and consciously navigating differently.

What will you do now that you didn't do before to help you progress and move forward? Suppose you do nothing and continue to avoid it, pretending it didn't happen. You may stunt your growth because you'll keep encountering something that reminds you of the past, leads you back to that issue, or you might withdraw completely, leading to feelings of inadequacy.

Sometimes, you must shift your perspective, view things differently, and adopt a new approach. Spiritual human behavior involves taking a fresh approach to tackle longstanding issues, not only within the individual but also within the community, the country, and the world.

Spiritual human behavior is how your soul develops and influences your daily behavior. So, when I say that you may lack, I mean that you may lack certain wisdom or understanding. You might not be able to do something because of an unresolved issue that remains unaddressed within you.

You may have forgiven the person or situation. You may have done everything else to ensure you're not holding back anyone and are not connected to anyone else in unforgiveness. But have you forgiven yourself? Have you taken the time to heal or focused on more than just healing? Have you reflected on the choices that brought you to where you are? Whether you like that place or not, addressing the things that will help you transform into who you're meant to be is essential. Spiritual human behavior emphasizes the spirit/mind, heart/soul, and body, which serve as the vehicle for your soul's mission.

The primary aim of this theory is to address the challenges that hinder individuals from maturing and growing with age, as well as developing on a meaningful level alongside their growth. Spiritual human behavior directly addresses the issue of confronting soul-level challenges- the things you run from, avoid, or feel too afraid to face because you don't want to deal with them, don't want to think about them or find it challenging to arrive at a solution.

We take the time to help you learn how to break down possible problems, identify them, and fix them within yourself based on desired results.

We hope you find yourself in this book and use it as a tool to grow all the days of your life. Enjoy!

Table of Contents

This book describes spiritual human behavior and represents just one part of a broader picture of faith, human behavior, and human nature. It illustrates how all these elements of this world work together to help you grow and evolve as a person. It consists of 7 sections and 11 chapters.

Your soul lives in this body and operates from the depths of your mind. With all we know, let's help others understand the basics of spiritual human behavior and spiritual human development. No matter where you come from or where you are, you can develop into the highest spiritual being, accessing true oneness in the human body and helping others to understand who they are as souls in this human body.

  Section 1: Establishing the Journey
        Chapter 1: How the Mind Works.
        Chapter 2: The Will of God.
        Chapter 3: Parental Influences.

Section 2: Spirituality without Religion (How All Things Work Together)
        Chapter 4: God's Provision System & Free Will.
        Chapter 5: The Holdover Theory.

Section 3: What's Expected from Self and Others
   Introduction: Call The Bluff Theory & Other Factors
   Chapter 6: The Band-Aid Effect (Exploring Defense Mechanisms)

Section 4: Clarity, Understanding, and Walking Your Path
   Chapter 7: The Judas Theory, A Lesson in Grace
   Chapter 8: The Spiritual Paradox Theory
   Chapter 9: The Deja Vu Theory

Section 5: Looking for a Sign
   Chapter 10: The Alignment Theory

Section 6: The Commission
   Chapter 11: The Light Worker Theory

Section 7: The Love Warranty

Within The Band-Aid Effect, you will also find insight into the mindset of gold diggers, manipulators, and womanizers, traits that we will identify and help you navigate through and deal with. Use this book as a tool to grasp the things that you know about yourself, to see what you're placing yourself around, your surroundings, and your environment. This is one baby step in the right direction to change your life forever.

Section 1:
Establishing a Foundation

Chapter 1: How the Mind Works

This chapter will explore the childhood experiences that shape your values, morals, and any religious beliefs you may hold. It is intended to be reflective as we examine childhood, helping us understand why we are who we are. This can be applied to the collective as you apply the thought process throughout your life.

Let's get right into it. Childhood experiences often shape life. The key to the theory of spiritual human behavior is reflecting on your feelings—whether you felt rejected, abandoned, misled, misguided, or experienced joy, peace, or excitement. All these feelings are important because you need to learn who you are, why you are that way, and what influenced you most. This will help you to understand your purpose and how to navigate life.

When you understand these aspects of yourself, you can realign the direction of your life and your actual goals. Everything we encounter in childhood influences us through our observations, experiences, lessons, and environmental context.

We must recognize and accept that when we enter this world, we inherently know nothing about what defines respectable individuals or personal values and morals. We don't know how to give, receive, show, and express love or understand hate. All we know when we are born into this world is that the person to whom we were born and given is the one we belong to, to an extent.

As a parent, your child doesn't recognize you as a mother until you define your role as a mother, mom, or mommy, whichever you prefer. You care for them, nurture them, and teach them how to handle emotions, understand different feelings, and manage them when interacting with others.

You are their first line of education from the moment they are newborns until they reach school age. They learn how to speak from you. As a parent, you should consider this when you have children. In this book, in this first chapter, we reflect on our childhood experiences as a means to heal and change our behavior patterns. Whether you are 10, 20, 45, or even 100 years old doesn't matter.

Some things you have been patterned to do are based on things you've been exposed to. A person who's been around nothing but love all their lives is more bound to be a loving person than someone who has been beaten, cursed out, hated on, or dealt with harshly. The person who has been dealt with harshly may begin to deal with people harshly.

The person who has been loved begins to love and love others in the way they have been loved, or even more. Reflect on each childhood experience. Birthdays- how did you enjoy them? Why didn't you enjoy them? What was good? What was bad? What was indifferent? Consider your first love, as well as your parental units, guardians, teachers, aunts, uncles, and grandmothers.

Who has impacted you most, and what have you learned from them? What lessons did you take from your mother? What insights did you gain from your father? In addition, reflect on your experiences with your mother, father, aunts, and uncles. Always remember that their experiences with you influence their interactions with their parents, relatives, friends, coworkers, employers, and the world around them. The goal, the hope, and the purpose are to establish strong foundations- positive, healthy foundations- where you begin to see results and understand precisely why you are achieving those results.

Your values are established during your childhood. What were you allowed to do? What were you not allowed to do? Do you remember why you weren't allowed to do certain things? Do you remember who corrected you? Do you remember who helped you? Who mentored you? Who did you look up to the most, and why? As a child, you have an outlook on things, but if you think about it as an adult, your views of a childhood experience might change.

In this process right now, what do you still value from those encounters, those relationships, those jobs- everything you've ever experienced? Who taught you? How did they teach you? Was it effective? Did it help you grow? Did anyone assist you in learning how to establish boundaries for yourself or balance a checkbook? It's all Fundamental and influences how you perceive yourself and the world around you.

These answers help you identify areas for improvement. The best way to address an undesirable pattern is to find its root cause and consider how and where it should be changed. If you find yourself attracted to a specific romantic interest, ask yourself why that attraction exists. What kinds of people were present during your upbringing that influenced your choices regarding not only whom you attract but also whom you are willing to respond to, give a chance, or allow to invest their time in you, as their time is just as valuable as yours? However, it is essential to understand precisely why.

Why do you find that appealing? What attracts you to that type of person? This can be profound, but it can also be daunting. It's akin to delving into the depths of your soul.

What made you want to dress that way or adopt that style? Have you ever desired attention from someone? If so, from whom? How was that need satisfied? Has it been satisfied? How do you ensure you're not in the same situations you disliked in the past?

Now think about religion, as it is one of those aspects of life that is learned. You don't enter the world knowing about God, the Bible, or what to support or oppose. Those are concepts you are taught. Children who are not taught what is good or bad often wonder why. It is not just that something is good or bad, but why is it considered good or bad? This understanding helps you know why you're making your choices and decisions.

Childhood is essential to overall development, despite how eventful it is. If you've witnessed your mother making poor decisions, you will repeat those poor choices or reflect on her decisions to determine how to create better experiences as your experiences flow from your choices.

How do you choose the people you surround yourself with today, as an adult, teenager, or even a child? What did you permit? What were you compelled to allow to happen to you, around you, or whatever the case may be? Now, when I mention this, think about friendship. When you were a child, were you required to share your toys? Even with those who treated you poorly, were you expected to be kind to individuals who abused, manipulated, or used you?

As you get older, reflect on how you learned to structure relationships. How did you learn discipline? Who taught you the values and the morals that you need to be established as a responsible adult?

Understanding your childhood experiences starts with knowing who you are, where you are, and where you feel vulnerable. Also, where do you feel comfortable? Your vulnerabilities can help you just as much as your comfort. To avoid vulnerability, you must examine, explore, and discover the factors that genuinely make you vulnerable.

Do you know why you move, operate, think, act, embrace, accept, or reject different things? Do you understand why you do the things you do? Everything you do today can be connected to a childhood experience. Everything you think, conceptualize, and comprehend in your mind stems from and is subtly rooted in how you were taught and how you learned to handle problems as a child.

In some ways, the people you are attracted to will resemble those you respect or those around you during childhood.

In most cases, you limit yourself to the type of people around you, regardless of whether you think you're better or could do better. If drug dealers surround you, then you may be drawn to those living that lifestyle because you were raised and adapted to it. If you were born into a close-knit family that supported one another, nine times out of ten, you are likely to believe in close-knit companionship and brotherly and sisterly love as you grow older.

If you were a loner, then nine times out of 10, as you get older, you will still be a loner, not lonely, a loner. Being lonely means being uncomfortable with yourself when you're by yourself. Being a loner means being comfortable with yourself, whether people are around you or not.

Most loners find joy in books and self-sufficient activities. If you are an only child or were raised as one, you know how to be self-contained. In contrast, being alone might be challenging if you come from a large family since you're accustomed to having many family members around. You enjoy built-in friendships and various interactions.

Your mind operates based on every experience you've had, everything you've encountered, and each like, dislike, hurt, bruise, joy, and wonderful moment. At this moment, everything you've experienced in life, from birth to now, has contributed to the person you are today. Until age 15, you were shaped by those around you. They helped you learn, grow, and develop, providing education about the world.

They should also help you understand who you are as a person. If they haven't, we are here to help.

Chapter 2: The Will of God

This is one of those chapters that I like to explain, as everything happens for a reason. When you talk about the will of God, it makes me first think about the Bible, which tells us that before we were born, God knew who we were. Before we were formed in our mother's wombs, God knew us, that he is the author and finisher, and that he knew everything we would do before we got here.

If that's the case, then there are no mistakes that you could have ever made. Whether you think it's a mistake or people have made you feel like you could have done something different or done things better. Aside from being in jail and committing crimes voluntarily, there are no mistakes because God knew you before you came.

He knows the amount of hair that you are going to have. He knew if you were going to be bald. He knew that you would meet that boy in high school or that girl in college.

He knew that I would get married and have children. Before it happened, he knew I would get a divorce, but he also knew that those things would grow me and help me to encourage you.

This is the thought process I've had to adopt with everything I've experienced. If you have not read my book, It's My Time, please do so to see how Chamone Adams overcame some of life's most challenging situations.

In every experience, I learned to think about it as if God allowed me or sent me to earth to endure this difficulty so that I could help somebody else in the next generation without going through something. Nothing I've ever done that was challenging, trying, or overwhelming was by mistake.

Just think about it. If you changed just one millisecond of anything, your life could be different for better or worse.

If your life isn't where you would like it to be, this is your opportunity to change how it goes from this point on. If you're reading this book, you are at a turning point. You are here right now, reading, because you are curious about how to get to the next level.

Not just get to the next level in business and life, but also learn how to change and influence your soul in a way that allows others to grow from your growth. So think about it. How could you make a mistake when God planned your life? How could you think something going differently would be better than where you are?

Later in the book, we'll discuss the paradox and learn how to make better decisions. But here, we're just establishing the foundation. You are not a mistake.

Everything in your life has a purpose. Everything has had a lesson behind it. You have to look for the lesson. That lesson becomes a blessing. You may have experienced a bad relationship, but when you find the lesson, you will see it's a blessing.

You didn't finish school, or didn't enjoy learning traditionally. What have you learned from the trials, tribulations, and every experience you've had up to this point? If something ends in a result you dislike, start at that point and see where changes can be made so that you can alter the course of your future by changing how you view your history. How can you use the information from the previous chapter to help change your outlook on life?

Everything you've been through has conditioned you to get where you should be. How do you look at things that seem like mistakes or challenges? How do you view life? How have those things changed how you think about things and how you handle yourself moving forward? Sometimes, things may seem overwhelming.

When you examine the core basis of those factors, you can understand how to progress and move forward. You can reflect on situations where you might feel you made a mistake, return to that moment, and learn from what you once perceived as a mistake.

If you met the wrong person, began dating, and took that person seriously, then it blew up in your face. What red flags did you see that would have caused you to halt or have caution in moving forward that you ignored, and you decided that the red flag wasn't more important than the person, the situation, the experience, or whatever the case may be?

We go through some things to teach, guide, help, and mold us. But you have to see every single portion of your life as purposeful. Every time that you've been abused, ask yourself, What did you learn from that? How do you not put yourself in a situation moving forward to be put back in an abused state of mind and environment? Because abuse is a state of mind, once you get used to being treated a certain way, you think that's okay.

You believe it's acceptable, and you're okay with it. It doesn't matter if it's acceptable or okay or if you feel good. It's what you've been conditioned to learn to accept.

It goes back to what I said. How many times have you been forced to do something despite how the people treated you? You're forced to be friends. You're forced to talk.

You're forced to do things, but you're not forced to learn why you do it. You don't understand or learn how to comprehend what's going on.

You learn to deal with it. The reality is that we have to learn from situations, not just deal with them. Too often, we are forced to deal with situations instead of learning why we are in them and how to get out of them.

If we feel uncomfortable in a situation or feel we are being used or manipulated, we should look for ways to avoid making the same mistake again. I've found that many people rush from one situation to another.

It doesn't matter if it's a relationship, a job, an educational field, or a person; instead of stopping and pausing, especially if you believe it was a mistake, remember that there is no such thing as mistakes.

If you feel something went wrong or you could have done better, stop and reflect on everything. What could you have done differently? What would you do differently if given the chance to do it over again?

If you didn't learn from the first situation, it will return. You can either address and learn from it or be in the same situation again. It may involve a different person, a different place, or a different job. If the mentality of the situation and how you handle it hasn't changed, you're still in the same predicament; it's just with another person, job, or place.

It's almost as if a person moves out of town but doesn't make any other changes. No matter where you go, you're always going to be there. No matter where you go, you'll always have to put some effort into whatever you're doing. No matter where you go, you're going to have to learn how to establish yourself, how to have control and responsibility, how to be a good steward, how to cook, how to clean, how to take care of yourself, and how to take care of your children if you have them.

Think back to your childhood experiences. This ties into how the mind works because anything from your childhood experiences is also a part of your path. So you now have to go back to those childhood experiences, grab a notepad, and write them down.

If you have the workbook, great.

If not, get some paper until you can invest in the workbook.

Write down those experiences.

Write down each good and bad experience and what you learned from it, because some of those things you even saw, dealt with, or were around as a child will come back to you to see if you learned how to overcome them.

Those things will replay in your life until they've been overcome. Generational curses are not what you think: my grandmother's, her sister's, or her brother's, or the kids—the mother, the brother— have them. No, generational curses are not my child's or their child's doing. It's the responsibility of the family's elders to address negative behavior patterns until they're broken and until they're healed.

It can't be broken until you confront your struggles, until you examine the things you thought were mistakes to figure out at what point you began to feel like it, or when it started to feel like it was not a good idea. Because when you feel a certain way, you need to understand why you feel that way. Some of this is just introductory psychology, so you can connect your feelings with an action, a reaction, or how you handle the situation. The goal here is not to avoid any negative experiences, but to learn from every negative situation, allowing it to foster a positive outlook on life.

Chapter 3: Parental Influence

Your decisions today can be influenced by the choices made by your parents. We've already touched on this topic a bit, but let's delve a little deeper. When I mention parental influences, I mean what you observed from your parents? What type of love did you receive from them? What kind of encouragement did you experience? What vacations did you go on with your parents? What examples did they set for you? The critical thing about parental influence is that we should not look down on our parents, but learn from their lives.

This is not for you to judge your parents because they have experienced life based on what they grew up knowing, how they were taught, how they learned, and how they coped. Your parents either taught you what they knew, what they learned, or what they were accustomed to, although sometimes they teach you from the things they prayed to experience.

This illustrates the role of parental influences in establishing a foundation and the basic principles of one's morals, values, and religious beliefs.

The theory suggests that you will either be exactly like your parents or completely different from them. However, this theory varies significantly because each area is unique. You may resemble your mother, but you might not behave like her.

You may plan like your dad, but execute like your mother. If your parents experimented with drugs, you may have witnessed the causes, effects, and the damage that drug and alcohol use inflicted upon your parents, or any other destructive behaviors they engaged in that were addictive.

You may decide, "I do not want that lifestyle." You may handle certain portions of habit-forming activities better because you understand how they changed your parents' lives or what you've observed from them.

For instance, I hate the smell of alcohol. Oh my God, it just makes me sick to my stomach. The reason why, though, is that when I was younger, I remember the stench of bars and alcohol that lingered when a person came home after partying. I used to have to clean up brown liquor vomit, and that left an imprint on me. So now I don't drink much.

I used to be a heavy drinker in the military when I was still struggling to find myself and feel accepted. Then I realized that I needed to change when I noticed my drinking heading toward a place I didn't like or one I'd seen others experience. I managed to stop, take control, and essentially avoid a terrible addiction altogether. Nowadays, I might drink when I'm out, but I prefer to drink in social settings, such as when I'm trying to relax or when I'm dating someone and we share a drink or something.

Aside from that, I completely stay away from alcohol. I can smell when someone has had a beer or liquor. Even if it was just one or two drinks, my nose detects and picks it up, which upsets my stomach.

I'm not saying this as someone who was around alcoholics or that anyone in my family lost their life to alcoholism. Being around people who look like they are having fun when drunk can have an impression on a child. If they are like me, that impression could lead a child to follow in those footsteps, drinking or being out all the time, which could result in the smell of bars and alcohol or make them despise it so much that they can't even date someone who smells like bars and alcohol.

Parental influence is significant because, even though parents may advise you to follow their words rather than their actions, it is easy to make decisions based on the examples they set instead of their instructions. Therefore, it's essential to lead by example if you are to lead. Demonstrate how to do this, as it is very challenging to show someone how to be or do something if you are not embodying it yourself or cannot encourage them in their faith.

Let's be very clear: a parent who has never attended college can still encourage their child to pursue higher education. A parent who skipped college but became a millionaire through their efforts may be unable to persuade their child to attend college, as they have succeeded without it. Conversely, there are children whose parents attended college but are now deeply in debt and have never found careers they love. They merely took jobs to pay the bills, which could be miserable.

A child observes this and thinks, " I see that you went to college, but I see your misery, sadness, your unfulfillment, and maybe that's not what I want to do for myself." There are also those people who went to college, picked a major they love, explored options, and emerged from college with a career they adore that doesn't feel like a job, working, or anything adverse.

When they go to where they work, what they call their employment- whether it's self-employment or a job for someone else- they are fulfilled, happy, well-paid, and have a family that loves them, and whom they love.

A person who has parents with those qualities in life- not just money, but also a sense of joy, happiness, and fulfillment- is more likely to have a child who goes to college because the example set was one of going to college and being happy, established, having ownership, setting an example, and being a leader.

You can also learn from a person who works hard, who is punctual, caring, and loving.

A child in need of love who never feels it will either become a person very needy for love, grasping at every opportunity for affection. Conversely, they can develop into a child who learns not to love, lacking the knowledge to show love and express emotions appropriately, because they have never been taught to do so. They may not have witnessed their mom or dad expressing their feelings or being loving toward someone. If a child never sees their parent with a companion or mate, that could leave them scarred if they're never made to understand why they're single.

It's almost like being a divorced person. You should try to help your children understand why the divorce happened. One, so that they never question if it was because of them or something they did that caused the divorce.

Children should understand the essential qualities of being present in a relationship when they marry. For instance, the other day, my son and I discussed that he cannot just run out or storm off when he gets into an argument with his sister. The worst thing a man could ever do is run out on a woman when she's upset, angry, or trying to express herself. It's best to stop, listen to what she's saying, understand her perspective, and then work together to reach a mutual understanding or agreement, ensuring that the issue will not arise again, rather than running away or avoiding the situation.

The experience taught me the importance of being present, addressing issues, not allowing people to treat me any way, and not conforming to a specific shape or persona. Suppose you're in an environment where you cannot witness love among people or feel love and embrace positivity. In that case, you need to learn to be yourself, accept yourself, love yourself, and discover the steps required to become who you wish to be.

Learn to embrace who you are, what you like, and what draws your interests. You see, life is deep. It's deeper than what many people make it out to be.

Everything you've experienced prepares you for where God intends to lead you. Every situation you encounter should teach you a lesson. Every unfavorable experience should help you grow; you need to examine what occurred, how you reached this point, and whether you could change it to improve your situation from where you currently are. Since second chances are not always available, what would you do moving forward from today?

Reflecting on this first section of spiritual human behavior, can you see how you've grown from childhood to adulthood? Do you recognize the areas in which you've learned and adapted over time that you would like to change? Spiritual human behavior involves learning to embrace yourself on a soul level so that your human behavior reflects your true self as a soul, aligned with your purpose on earth.

This book is designed to help you understand yourself so that you can grow into the best version of yourself that God has ever imagined. You were created with a purpose, at this time, for a reason. Everything you've ever lived through was designed to grow and prepare you. Now, the question is, how has this reflection helped you? Please grab a piece of paper and a pen, and listen again if needed. Begin to jot down things you remember that influenced and changed your thought process.

When you were growing up, you used to be a certain way. On this day, something happened, and it changed the way you perceive things. Write down everything that has changed your perception that you can remember.

Doing this may arouse or awaken other memories, and that's good because the goal is to examine your life to see the lesson in each thing you've endured and how that is a true blessing. It's not a mistake; how you were raised was so you could become who God created you.

Your parental influences help develop you by showing you what you value. What's important to you? If you experienced something during your childhood or teenage years, or if you observed traits in your parents or others that you didn't like, how did you become different? This book aims to help you become an individual in a world of people trying to be like others. Don't seek out what someone else should do or how they do it.

Understand the reasons behind your actions. Today is the day to reflect on anything troubling you, evaluating thoughts that come to mind, regardless of whether they cause pain or bring healing. Consider when you noticed a change. What aspects of that situation impacted you positively or negatively? Regardless of the outcome, reflect on your experience.

Think about your childhood friends. Think about elementary school. Think about what you were taught to accept.

All of these things are very important as we move on to the following sections of this book. Can't wait for you to catch up.

Section 2: The Understanding
Creating Framework and Structure

Chapter 4: God's Provision System & Free Will

Finding your path is similar to accessing a GPS. "God's Provisional System" guides you forward and through life.

Consider what I just said about moving forward in life. Then, reflect on what I mentioned regarding the GPS. A GPS, God's Provisional System, offers you options.

Note: The belief is that you are a soul in heaven, outside of this realm of existence, meeting with God before you are born to select your life's experiences. God appoints each soul for their experience on Earth with a purpose and mission to which their soul must awaken.

If the Bible is true when it says, " Before you are formed in your mother's belly, God knew you," then it's safe to say there is an understanding on a soul level with God.

God knew everything about you: the hairs on your head, everything you would do, every good place, every bad place. If that's true, then free will is like a GPS. I don't mean to belittle free will or your ability to navigate life as desired.

Starting from point A and aiming for point B with God's provisional system gives you direction.

It's almost like building a house; the blueprint is provided. There are options for constructing the structure. You can use various types of beams and pressure-treated wood, similar to the different routes in God's provisional system on a GPS that guides you to your destination. Before you leave point A, you have a plan: the will of God for your life.

You're given that, your blueprint. Before you even get to Earth and entered your mother's womb, what had to take place to bring you there is what brought your mom and dad together. For some, this can be challenging to accept, depending on who you are and how you were conceived.

But for others, this could be a sigh of relief because within it, one must understand that sometimes miracles require unplanned events. What do I mean by that? Occasionally, for miracles to manifest, actions that are spontaneous or appear spontaneous at the time must happen for the outcome. As we explained in the previous chapters, everything in your life was already written for you, just like everything happens for a reason.

If that's the case, then a one-night stand could have been a miracle because you needed to be created for something particular to happen. If nothing in life is outside God's knowledge, we must view life differently. That's where God's provisional system and "free will" come into play.

There is no free will in the sense that you can come here and do whatever you want on Earth. I don't believe that is the case. I believe that when you are in heaven, before you are formed in your mother's womb, there is a soul plan designed for you, whether it's one that you are continuing or one that you are starting anew.

If it's a new soul plan, the soul is fresh, or has never been on Earth in this form. That soul has come to Earth for the first time. And then, when they die, they will, quote unquote, reincarnate.

When I say reincarnate, they will leave their physical body. Their soul will experience physical death here on Earth in whichever way they signed up before coming to Earth. So when you come to Earth, everybody comes to Earth to die, essentially.

There is no living being or soul that leaves Earth alive in the physical body in which they came. If there is such a thing as reincarnation, it speaks to the freedom of beliefs that your soul lives on to finish out whatever it came to begin.

Once your body physically dies in your first lifetime, you may go back to heaven and receive a different portion of your assignment. In the belief system of speaking freedom, there is also a possibility that your soul, before coming to Earth in your current physical body, is given a list of what your soul is going to accomplish in your lifetime.

Technically, Earth is merely a part of God's Kingdom.

The kingdom of God encompasses the entire universe. Some locations within the universe are a light year away, while others may be four or five light years away.

What is a light year? I am not going to discuss that here right now. Just know that a year in space differs from what you hear, experience, and see here on Earth. God, the source of all things, exists beyond space.

If you are a person who believes the Bible, it states that one day with God is like a thousand elsewhere. So, imagine if one day on Earth is equivalent to a thousand years in terms of God's perspective in the universe. Additionally, a light year is a measure of a thousand years.

That's deep. But let's continue.

When you're in the heavenly realms with God, the source and creator, and commit to a task before you arrive here, you are destined to remember it once you get to Earth.

Imagine that you are informed of the options, obstacles, defeats, and stress before you arrive. You are shown everything you will experience in each lifetime. This occurs in every lifetime presented to you, as you are given an overview of your entire life cycle.

Each lifetime has sections, much like these books.

Life Cycle & Numbers

Let's say your life cycle number is seven.

If you investigate or explore life cycles, the life cycle you are currently in as a soul shapes your experiences. With nine life cycle numbers, based on your birth date, you can determine the life cycle your soul has assigned itself to. You might question why I mention numbers only going up to nine, considering there is certainly a 10.

Well, there is a 10. But technically speaking, 10 is just one all over again. So you go 1, 2, 3, 4, 5, 6, 7, 8, 9, and 10.

Then you go to 19 and then 20, which is two again. If you take any number and add it to nine, you will get that number again for a second time. So five plus nine is 14.

The digits of 14 added together equal 5. So it's just 5 a second time, but with the nine. Regarding the number system, this will make it into an entirely different book.

As we just stated, the number system goes from one through nine. But if you take nine and add it to any number, it will still be that number. So, knowing how to look at numbers differently to see what they are will teach you a lot of different things.

So 26 is eight. 42 is six. 135 is nine.

It's just presented differently, in a shape and form. So if you're not knowledgeable about numbers and the strength, dominance, and responsibility that comes with numbering, you will not notice that all of these numbers are still one through nine, or give any thought to it. In your mind, you've been programmed and conditioned to think that every number is a different number instead of taking a moment to consider whether this equals that, or that equals this.

I've been personally interested in numbers since I was a child.

Let's get back into God's Provisional System and Free Will.

You have your options. You have a quick way. You have a less-lit way, meaning you may get on a highway and experience fewer lights, but it may not be the fastest way to get there on the GPS.

We all know that GPSs can be delayed. They can calculate things that you do not see, things that you are unaware of. Depending on how fast you can get, comprehend, and move through the route you've been given, it can sometimes prolong the trip.

That's how life is. You can't stray from a course. Free will is okay; God, you've given me this life course, this destiny. To reach this destiny, there are 10 routes I could take. Some paths among those routes might lead to dead ends, literally or figuratively. There may be tough times on one route, either literally or figuratively.

You might run out of gas on this route, literally or figuratively. In this route, you may need help or directions. Sometimes, even with GPS, you may need confirmation of directions.

For example, it directs you to take a specific route, but the instructions can be vague due to road improvements or changes in the scenery. It may indicate a particular point that could have been reconfigured or reconstructed and might not be updated on the GPS, but it's essential to stop and ask for guidance along the way.

This is foundational, pivotal, and life-changing because if you view your life as a GPS and consider free will as having options. Option one is straight and narrow, while option two may have a few curves.

It may take you to places where you could see some things you would not see on option one. Option three could take you through the mountains and valleys, and it would be a beautiful experience overall. But during those mountains and valleys, it may not seem like you will ever get there because of how the route is laid out.

Take a moment to think. A fourth option might be a rural road that offers a back way. It's not on the GPS because it's not a conventional street, but it could still lead you to that path. You might see a choice that directs you one way but includes some unfamiliar areas that it cannot display specifically. If you follow this route, you may reach your destination, although the duration remains uncertain.

The GPS may lose connection on the way, and you will have to use your map to get there.

This may be completely over your head, and that's fine. But think of your GPS. If you have a cell phone and you're reading this book, get on your cell phone and open your GPS.

In time, it'll make sense. No, really.

Please put it in a location or your last location. About 10 years ago, if you were using a GPS and it lost signal, didn't have the route, or something was off, you needed a map.

You needed a separate map because the GPS was changed. If it wasn't updated, you may not have received the new course that's been provided, and maybe a road was closed.

Perhaps there is a detour due to construction. If you're using a phone today, enter an address and check your GPS. There are many ways to reach your destination. The route you choose can affect your outcome, and you might encounter a dead end. You could face a dangerous area, a detour, a roadblock, or a checkpoint. Free will allows you to choose your path and the options related to your destination. The destination is the goal.

How you decide to accomplish the goal presents you with options in itself.

Consider the options for starting a business. You can collaborate with a business builder that provides a community or resources featuring various ideas and strategies for launching a business. Alternatively, you can do the legwork and generate ideas and strategies for achieving your business goals.

When considering the construction of a new home, depending on how your loan was approved, you can hire a contractor to create blueprints that match your desires. Alternatively, you can be unconventional; you might choose a mobile home you select, position it wherever you wish, and purchase land. The options for home building are unlimited.

Apply that same thinking to Freewill. Once you come to Earth, you have been given a purpose. The course or option you take to obtain that purpose determines your result.

You might attend school, or you might not. You might establish a business, or you might not. You can pursue a job, or you might not. You might become an actor, or you might not. You might live as a street thug, or you might not. You could choose to be a doctor, or you might not. You could opt to be a father, or you might not.

Once you get on Earth, everything you do will fall within the parameters that will lead you to that course, that option. There's a destination, regardless of whether you realize it. Some may sign up for a lifetime to be short, while others may sign up for a longer one. Speaking Freedom has no theory on who decides or what determines how long someone lives here on Earth.
The time someone has on Earth may be predetermined within their soul contract, which they come to Earth with for a purpose. It could be based on an option that leads to a dead end. Many factors could influence it. For some, their lives are stolen because they didn't receive the update in the GPS to inform them, not that way. This way today. No, not those people. These people. No, not that job. This job. No, not that service. Get this service.

It's getting more profound and more serious as I elaborate. Imagine not going against your inner voice and trusting the calm, even when you don't understand where it's taking you. These books are designed to help you think better, learn, grow, evolve, and do better.

If you get a better train of thought on how you see what God has created you to be, you can live better. You'll be able to love better. So when you think about free will, don't think, God, let me do whatever I want to within a specific parameter, because if you get outside of that course, you will never meet your destination.

If you step outside that course, you may never experience some things that God designed for you because free will is an option. Option one, option two, option three. You may have a hundred thousand options before you, but not all will be as appealing when you understand your purpose.

Not all options will be enticing, depending on the values instilled in you. The choices available may vary based on how your brain functions. We often think of free will as the ability to do whatever we want rather than as a matter of choosing a path, but that's not entirely accurate.

Free will is a matter of the course you decide to take when doing something, but it's essential to understand that this course doesn't change the assignments you're meant to experience in this lifetime. It simply alters the path and assignments intended for your life. This allows your soul to learn, grow, and reach the long-term goals it's designed to achieve.

You may be appointed to experience certain things. Then, when you are appointed to experience certain things, you may change the environment very well. You may be taken from one place and placed in another, but you'll still have to overcome some struggles.

You're still going to have to manage your thinking. You will still have to do many things, even though you changed the environment, because your assignments are your assignments. It doesn't matter what course you're on or the path you try to take to avert the inevitable. If your purpose was to be a doctor, you might not get a medical degree, but you will find yourself caring for sick people.

It doesn't matter what the environment is. You must do essential things in life that will help you evolve. These actions will contribute to your growth and reignite what's within your soul.

That's the part you're waiting for, anticipating receiving once you change course. Your surroundings only alter the environment. How do you move forward? Which path in God's provisional system will you take?

Returning to our home-building example, when you narrow down your options, whether you prefer a builder or a private contractor, which builder do you want to choose?

Now you have to figure out the option and the floor plan. One builder could have five different floor plans. In this sense, a builder is a metaphor that can be your friends, peers, pastor, yourself, parents, or anybody who influences or helps you build the life you desire to live. Just like you can have various options for which course to take on your journey here on Earth, the goal is to feel fulfilled.

The amount you can borrow if necessary determines the result. It depends on how you manage your assignment and the choices you make. Now, you can maximize your home. You can enhance your life and how you live it, achieving everything you desire based on what you're willing to create.

The question: Does what you want match what you've been approved for? If you're getting a loan, does it match your existing sole contract? Because the options that you see in the house, such as a model home, may not be something you can afford based on what you were pre-approved for. Remember you are the temple carrying a purpose connected to the oneness in all people.

This relates to counting your costs, understanding your purpose, recognizing what you've been strengthened and shaped for, and then identifying your desires and their origins. Most of this derives from learning, knowing, and loving yourself.

Embracing free will here on earth guides the GPS that charts the route you should take as you align with God's frequency through prayer. We now have choices: hire a builder in a community to construct five or ten homes, or observe how God manifests in another person's life.

Once you choose your blueprint, there's more. You must select the floors and decide on the colors for your walls based on the cost, approval, and the amount you can afford.

Before deciding on any path, education, career, job, or goals, you should ask God for a purpose. Go within yourself. If you do not believe in God, and you happen to get this book as an atheist, thank you very much for purchasing it.

Explore your inner self; delve deeper into what you consider the source of all things, and inquire why you were placed on Earth and given that family. Ask for guidance, strength, clarity, knowledge, and everything you need and desire, so that when it's time to move forward, you can already understand what it would cost to get you there. And let God surprise you along the way.

Before building a home, you must understand what you're approved for. You must know what options are available to you and which are not. You could choose a larger home with fewer options and later make adjustments, or opt for a smaller home with more features. It has everything, but will you eventually need to move to meet your future needs if you haven't already begun evolving your soul? Free will is about choices.

Do you take the easy course or the challenging one? Do you do more or less? Or do you find a balance or something entirely new? Do you get your updates? Do you speak to God regularly? Do you converse with the source consistently and ask the source, ask God, okay, what's new? What's changed? What's happening? Because everything you do affects someone, whether you realize it or not.

This is where prayer comes into play. How do I adjust to continue to reach the things I deeply desire in the depths of my heart and soul? Understanding who you are, why you are, and where you are to understand where you are going is pivotal. Imagine being the creator of your own life. What do you want out of life? Not the material things, not the easy-to-get things.

Unless you only want easy things, you will have to put in some work, especially on your soul. What do you desire? What speaks to your soul? What are your desired outcomes and expectations of life? Free will is the path, with the course to get there offering easy, challenging, and neutral routes.

If you go the challenging route, it's like going on an unpaved road with no upkeep in the middle of nowhere, trying to watch your step as you navigate the terrain. You don't know what's going to happen. You don't know what's coming.

All you know is that it's a way to get there, like faith, almost. You can learn the most about yourself on the dirtiest, darkest path. It's almost like going through hell because you're going through every hard time.

You're staying wrapped up in every challenging experience, but it will cost you. What's the price you're willing to pay for what you say your heart desires or what you want? What cycle will you remain in to keep those things? If you knowingly take the most challenging route to get there, even if it does nothing for you, free will allows you to stay on whatever course you choose while having the option to select a different course at any point. See, the neutral path is the straight and narrow.

You may experience some things, but never stray too far from the path. Eventually, you might discover the super-easy path where you're doing everything right, and all that could go your way is indeed going your way, with every possible assistance available.

In the most challenging times, you may find yourself stuck in a cycle, continually repeating the same patterns instead of making better decisions to help you break free. This is free will, allowing you to continue down that path. Every decision you make serves a greater purpose, as it can either help advance your journey or hinder it, potentially causing you to miss the awakening experience needed to achieve your goals.

The short end of the long is that free will does not mean you can do anything you desire, no matter what. It's the ability to choose the path you will be on and walk on amongst the options you're presented with. You're not presented with anything you want in the world.

You're presented with a soulful desire that encompasses your gifts, skills, talents, and grace for what you've been "assigned" to do, designed to guide you from where you are to where you believe, in your heart, you are meant to be. As your path can change dramatically with even a small decision, you will understand the power of free will. Imagine free will as a video game, perhaps Jumanji, where you start with a certain number of lives, and if you die in the game, you're given another life.

That's similar to someone who undergoes a near-death experience, which enlightens them about what to avoid and what not to do, helping them learn lessons about navigating their journey.

When you think about it, you can choose a course on video games. Not only can you select the course, but you can also decide the level and intensity, making it entirely up to you within those games.

It's your free will to choose which course and level you want to accomplish in video games. So imagine life like that. What if, by chance, you were living in a video game and everything you see is real on a physical, earthly dimension, but in your mind, you're still somewhere else? I'm not implying that something is wrong with you; rather, if you were in a video game, you would be a person observing yourself play the game. These new virtual reality games feel more real than ever.

Envision this concept. This is my view of free will. It leads me to consider that a soul might enter a body that wasn't meant for it or one it doesn't recognize as its own. Everything we do—according to the Bible or any religious text—implies that God knew us before we got here.

For God to have known us before our arrival, He would need to understand what we would face and experience here. We can only speak life into existence, make changes, learn from God, seek His guidance, and adjust our lives accordingly. For instance, growing up, I encountered several life-altering challenges, but one particularly stands out: when my mom attacked me and attempted to take my life.

That changed the course of my life. It made me start deciding things differently because I didn't have the same childhood or teenage years as most people. It made me become a better woman because I didn't have any resources.

That changed the course of my life. If I had not experienced that, I might not have joined the military or be here.

Most of the people that I went to school with or that I hung out with are either dead or in jail. I don't mean that they died of natural causes. Some of them had a sickness.

Most of them were killed. So, imagine if I had stayed in that environment, my test would have still been my test. I still would probably have children, but how many would I have? How much stress and struggle would accompany those things? These are just a few things to help you understand what I mean.

You've got two kids. One decides to join the NBA. The other decides to sell drugs.

Let's make it three. Another one starts selling drugs but then decides to go off to college and do something different. These three people could be from the same household, the same neighborhood.

They could be triplets, but each decision that is made will change the way that their course is set up. The person who's on the street selling drugs still has to face life-challenging decisions. They still have to provide for their family.

They still want to be loved and to be in a relationship. People who join the NBA or play professional sports also long for love. Often, they derive their sense of love from the affection received through sports.

For some, this dynamic can hinder their maturity compared to a different environment. When one acquires money and fame, and people regard you based on your achievements rather than your character, it can shift how others interact with you. Many will engage with you simply because you are a millionaire, solely due to your wealth.

They might not genuinely like or care for you, but they will continue associating with you because of your millions. Conversely, they wouldn't have anything to do with or tolerate you if you didn't possess millions.

The more successful you become, the more yes men surround you. Nowadays, an increasing number of individuals will critique and criticize you about aspects they likely couldn't handle themselves. The person involved in selling drugs shares a similar mindset to a basketball player, but they approach life differently.

They've decided that they don't want to put in that work or don't want to do what it takes to change where they are. They're comfortable with fast money and whatever girls come with it.

The reality is that a person in the NBA is not that much different from a person selling drugs. They have different career options, and their career options lead them to different courses in life.

Let's include the child who chose not to sell drugs and went to college. Ideally, those three individuals should collaborate because they can support each other's growth and development. The college student possesses the common-sense knowledge necessary to operate in the United States of America.

Does anyone understand what I'm saying? Not everyone acquires the knowledge needed to enter and understand enough to make changes based on what they recognize that people back home need. And that's crucial, if you ask me, but that's the point. Free will doesn't dictate this path.

It presents you with options. Free will does not force you to choose anything; it offers options.

It's an option when you prepare for a date. Nobody's forcing you to go on a date, but your choice should be: Do I know this person well enough? Is this person suitable? Can he protect me? Is she available for me to support? Is she submissive? I hope you're dating to marry or for a long-term relationship, not for short-term dating— no short-term dating, as it opens your heart to the risk of being broken.

But within free will, you get the option. You choose. What do you decide to do? Is that in alignment with your soul purpose? Do you feel the favor of God on your life while making those decisions? While you're moving that direction? Because honestly, when you're walking in a path of alignment with your soul and your heart is accepting, it changes everything.

You begin to see doors open. You begin to see people who come around that can supplement your life, whether they're supposed to be in your life for years, weeks, months, or days. There will be a difference when you begin to align with your purpose.

Now, back to the video game. When you're playing a video game, a course is already set. There is a way that you're supposed to go.

There is a way that doesn't seem right. Well, there is always a way that seems right. Nine times out of 10, in any video game, you have different options as well.

This option is the best analogy for free will. In a video game, you have options, okay? You choose the beginner's level, which is a straight course.

You don't have that many people that's fighting against you. It's easier when you don't have that many people fighting against you. It's the easy course because you've decided to go the easy route.

I can't determine the easy route for you because what may be easy for me may be hard for you. So it's hard to give examples of the easy route. For one person, selling drugs is the easy route.

For one person, going to school is the easier path. For another, being naturally athletic makes playing sports the simpler choice because that ability is inherent to them. It's their gift. It's their skill. These factors matter. Therefore, each person's path is influenced by their choices, decisions, and intensity levels, among other considerations.

Let's say you take the intermediate route.

On that path, I use the movie Jumanji as an example because in the latest version of it, a person was stuck in the game for 20-something years. In the original, it was a person stuck in the game for 20-something years. And this is so pivotal.

They were stuck because they didn't know. Well, one was stuck because he was down to one life left, after he tried to do the course on his own. But the course is not designed to be done alone. So he had to wait for someone to come and help support his efforts to win, to get out of the game.

Sometimes in life, you need that support system to progress, be great, and win the game. Now, this is the tricky part. Just imagine: what if you could choose your current life? What if none of this was by chance? What if you, before you were born in your mother's belly in the soul-dimensional atmosphere, decided that not only would you come to earth, but you would come to earth, and these are the parameters you would choose? The video game logic shows you that there will be some difficulties no matter what course you take. But even on each level, different paths can get you where you're supposed to be.

But guess what? If you mess up, you go back to the last accomplishment that you made. Then, you have to pick up from that last accomplishment you made and try to produce something more or something better. You must understand that you have the option of free will.

But it's only based on a specific parameter, depending on where you listen to this audiobook. Your choices could or could not include certain things. If you're from the "hood" or "the ghetto," then you don't have the same options as the queen of the UK.

Your free will is still distinct from everyone else's. Even two children growing up in the same household can have the same mother and father. However, the way their minds process life offers them different options.

One person may be good at one thing, and another may be good at another. The thing is figuring out yourself, learning your soul so that you can grow and be the best you can be. You can't make good choices and soul decisions if you don't know yourself.

This is one of the reasons it is essential for children to begin learning about self-love, finding their purpose, and connecting spiritually, not just in a religious sense, but in a way that fosters their growth and prosperity. This knowledge can help them develop self-confidence, withstand challenges, and make positive choices. Most people haven't been taught how to make good choices, so they may never reach their full potential because they don't understand how to choose growth over stagnation.

You must choose your purpose over stagnation, as your choices lead you to your destiny. Your destiny, in essence, is your soul opening up, making you available to learn and grow. It is not a person, place, or thing.

It's about realizing yourself and growing to the highest level of who you can be. We are influenced by various factors, such as our parents' desires, friends' wishes, peer pressure, social media, society, education, and historical truths. You need to break the barrier within you to discover what's best for you.

So you can learn your likes and dislikes. As a recap, we will go over what free will is. Free will is having a choice in the course or path you take along this journey.

Free will does not mean you can do whatever you want. You can, but your options depend on the parameters you were born into and those you create. The best circumstances and parameters you can establish come from self-discovery.

Self-discovery aligns you with what's good for you and what's not. It enables you to trust your intuition and soul, allowing you to unlock your full potential and achieve real growth. Allow God's provisional system, his GPS, and your inner knowing to guide you to the best version of yourself.

Chapter 5: The Holdover Theory

Just a brief recap: We've discussed how the mind works, childhood experiences, the will of God, everything happens for a reason, parental influence, decisions based on examples, free will, and God's provisional system. If you've listened to those, then that's great.

The Holdup Theory can be defined as when you get stagnant and something, someone, someplace, some circumstance, some thought process, or some hangup blocks you from moving on to your following blessing or lesson.

If this were a video game, you would have to complete a level, earn coins, and progress to the next one. The most challenging aspect of any video game is reaching the next level, whether it involves shooting something across the screen or competing against another player in a game. When there's a goal to achieve and you're striving to advance in the video game or life, there is a challenge, some opponent that tests your skills and allows you to move on to the next level.

Suppose another component allows you to advance to the next level in life, and it's holding you back. In that case, you may become stagnant in your thinking or interactions with others. You might experience a lack of motivation to finish something you said you wanted to do or something you need to do for yourself, whether it's taking care of your body, nurturing your mind, relaxing a little, or enjoying yourself and having a good time.

No matter what that test is, you don't have to go through something bad to obtain something good. However, you may have a lesson to learn to grow into your next level. Responding to that lesson can elevate you or set you back. It can strain your faith if you react negatively to a lesson meant to advance you or allow it to push you backward. If you don't see the challenge, look for the opportunity to learn something and try to teach it.

How do you determine if you're stagnant? If you're not growing at the same pace as the people around you, remember that your growth is not determined by anyone or anything else but by yourself. The more you seek to learn during challenging moments, the better equipped you will be to face whatever comes your way, rather than running from or avoiding the issues. This approach is essential for your self-esteem, life, and how you envision your success.

The hold-up theory comes in parts or phases because being held up means being challenged to do more to become better. That moment of challenge is where a lesson can be learned, whether it involves letting go of somebody, advancing in your knowledge, wisdom, understanding, health, mental capacity, or thought process. Whether getting another job, starting your own business, finding a career, being open to love, or adjusting your faith, trust, or love in yourself.

Recognizing what can hold you back from reaching your goals is essential. Regardless of your goals, whether finding a new relationship, a new home, fixing your credit, or anything else. There will always be a challenge, or rather, a test to see which decision you are willing to make. Being held up is very common.

It is not a state everyone remains in; most people can grow if they seek the knowledge, wisdom, or help they need to advance themselves mentally, spiritually, financially, physically, or in any other way they can imagine.

Your best lessons are learned when you're unhappy with your results. We will get into the first portion of being held up, which involves knowing the people around you.

Why do you have certain people around you? Do they align with your life purpose? Do they contribute to your overall growth? Will they support your development? Can you assist them in growing as well? Can you nurture each other to advance healthily in all areas of your life? This is not necessarily about romantic relationships.

This involves friendships, parental relationships, or any other platonic situation you are involved in. All of these things make a huge difference. We don't want to think that we must get away from our family, relatives, or the people we've grown up with all our lives, but sometimes, that is the inevitable way to grow.

Sometimes, planting and leaving it by the wayside is the inevitable way to grow. It's almost like an eagle. When eagles teach their children, they teach their eagle chicks/eaglets.

When eaglets are taught how to fly, they're taken to a high point and dropped so that their wings have the opportunity to work. There's no way to practice flying other than to fly.

When they're dropped from a high point, they are tested immediately. If they can't fly, their mother or father catches them. Whoever is above the flock catches them, and they continue doing this repeatedly.

Imagine that God is bringing lessons into your life to help you advance, learn more, go higher, and grow in every area. Consider the things that may hold that up. Again, you don't want to think about letting go of anyone.

Sometimes, you don't completely have to let go; you just need space to focus on what God has for you—what's best for you.

You shouldn't miss what's meant for you by getting caught up in what others cannot see for themselves. You might feel envious because you possess something or have abilities they lack. However, it's essential to surround yourself with people who continue to encourage you regardless, even if they lack those abilities.

Even if they don't have it, they encourage you anyway. You need to surround yourself with people who, if they have it, will treat you the same way you treat them. In balanced relationships, you know who you're dealing with, why you're dealing with them, and what they bring to the table. Those people have something to offer based on what you contribute as well.

The hold-up theory and understanding who's around you is critical because when you have the wrong people around you, you can be not involved in something yet still be accused of it just because of the type of people you associate with. Think about it for a second; take it all in.

The people around you will determine the direction of your life. You can either influence them, allow them to influence you, or mutually influence each other, leading to growth, decline, or stagnation. The hope is that you engage with these books, educate yourself, evaluate your environment, and consider the people you associate with to see if they help you grow.

According to Spiritual Human Behavior, your soul attracts people like you or those who need you. When attracting people like you, you allow them to demonstrate their similarity, support, and presence for you. However, being around the wrong people could hold you back.

They can also discourage you from pursuing relationships with people who are similar to you and have your best interests at heart. What's very important is that you figure out who you are. You read about this a couple of chapters ago, so you should've already been contemplating your identity, purpose, mindset, and why you are who you are.

Once you start thinking about why you are who you are and that everything happens for a reason, you can assess whether you are growing. Are people around you helping you grow at the pace you're supposed to? The goal is to avoid anything that distracts us or keeps us stagnant. You need to understand what it means to be held back, what it means to be stagnant, and what it means to allow God to grow, guide, and teach you through lessons learned, as opposed to repeating the same decisions repeatedly while wondering why nothing in your life is changing and why nothing good is happening.

You must evaluate the elements in your life today, how they arrived, and when. Does what keeps you from advancing relate to a childhood experience or something you observed growing up? How would you change based on the desires of your heart and what you truly want?

It is essential to understand the various distractions, why they are presented from a growth perspective, and what they might signify for your possibilities and potential. Know yourself first. Reflect thoroughly on where you wish to go. Know the controllable things.

What can you control about your environment? What can you control regarding the people around you? You cannot control the people around you, but you can control who you choose to have around you and the reasons for their presence. Do they serve a purpose? Do they support your purpose? Or are they there just for fun? Are they present simply because they can be, and you are engaged in something? Or are they there because you have nothing going on, which makes them feel better about their situation?

It's essential that you surround yourself with people who can feed you, how you can feed them, and who can help nurture your spirit the way you help nurture theirs.

If you're always around people who need your nurturing, guidance, and talking, I won't say you will be empty, but you will feel more drained because people are constantly leeching on what you have to offer, but they don't offer you anything. They have nothing, or if they offer you something, they try to get something instead of offering you something. To offer it, to help you grow, to help change your life, just a little.

But expect what you give and give what you expect. So if you expect people to treat you a certain way, then treat people that way. When you begin to give a certain level of treatment, care, and respect, you should also be able to expect that same thing back from those you keep around you, those who help feed you.

You shouldn't hang out every day with anyone who can't help feed you the way you feed them. No gossipers; they're a distraction. Social media is good if you're using it for positive purposes.

Even if you don't agree with everyone else, if you aim to help people learn, grow, succeed, and improve, you're winning. Helping others grow contributes to your growth.

Whatever you can help teach somebody else will promote your growth. Now, most people use those opportunities to help others, and while I won't call it a pyramid scheme, they leverage it as an opportunity to profit from somebody else's ignorance. It is profitable to sell your intellectual property, but it's also beneficial to help people without cost or at no charge.

Now, I'm not saying that this book will be free, and I'm not saying that I'll charge you a million dollars just to come and help you, either. Due to its popularity, it's easier to present something appealing and attract 100,000 listeners.

If you charge 100,000 people a dollar for some good information, you've already made $100,000. If each person tells two others, that's 300,000. Counting money is easy.

The mindset to keep it and to change can be a distraction. Spending on things that add no value to your life is also a distraction. When the money gets low, guess what? If you're only around people who think only about money, you'll get distracted because they're probably keeping up with the Joneses.

I don't know who the Joneses are, but they're probably keeping up with them and likely can't keep up. So they're doing more, spending more, and trying to look the part when they should be investing in living the part. You can look the part without living it.

You can appear to fill a role or look like you do something, but it could be the opposite, whether good or bad, happy or sad, productive or unproductive, creative or copycat. Still, you need to know who's around you, what's around you, and why. Some people are only there for a season.

You have people there for a reason, and then you have people there for a lifetime. And lifetime people are usually the people who have the same soul vibe as you.

People who relate to you and help you grow and challenge you, in any case. Not people who see you have something going on and tell you yes to everything. But people who don't push their beliefs on you either.

They are happy to see you grow because they're growing themselves. They will tell you what they think, but they won't try to force you to do what they would do. You need to have people around you who can nurture your soul the way you can nurture theirs, as well as mentors, if they are available.

However, the best mentor is someone who can also listen and learn from you. They will respect you for what you bring to the table, and you can respect them for what they contribute. Respecting each other for what you bring creates a solid foundation for growth. Everyone around you should be growing.

Anything alive is growing. Whether we realize it or not, growth is the goal in our minds, hearts, souls, and every aspect of life, in every possible way. Now, are the people in our lives here for a season, a reason, or a lifetime? Seasonal people may enter your life to help you reach a certain level or gain an understanding.

Once you reach that understanding, you're released from those individuals because it's time for both of you to grow to the next level. Everything ties in; all aspects of life are interconnected.

Everything in life ties in? What do you mean? Everything in life is tied in the sense that all things work together. If you are waiting for something and it is delayed by someone else, it does not just throw you off. It throws off whoever was waiting for you to do whatever you needed to reach your destination. If that makes sense, everyone in your life affects your life. The people around you affect you.

That's your dimension of living. Every person, every encounter you have, and everyone who comes near is at a specific time in their lives when they were meant to cross your path. Whether that is to help you reach a certain point or serve as a check marker—like in the matrix of life—there is a reason you encounter the people you do and are exposed to things at the times you are.

Please don't assume I'm only referring to people when I mention season, reason, and a lifetime. You might need to live somewhere for a season. You could have to work at a job somewhere for a season.

That season of being there could teach you something more related to your purpose than merely having that job. However, the experience is necessary to grow and reach where you need to go. Being a finance counselor at an online school for about a year has prepared me to be here.

That preparation helped me understand my vocation and what I enjoyed doing. I loved being on the phone and assisting people in clarifying their goals and motivations in life, rather than making hasty decisions based solely on financial opportunities. If you pursue something just for money and then accumulate debt, you're digging yourself in a deeper hole.

That door of opportunity, that season of me working at that school, prepared me. It allowed my mind to venture and see what I could do and how to change the world one person at a time. It also showed me as a team how working together brings all things together. But that was for a season.

Those people were for a season. I learned those things in that season that prepared and propelled me into what was to come. I could sit around and talk to Mormons and understand their livelihood and how things work for them.

I saw how living in Arizona differed significantly from the East Coast. I experienced California and the West Coast in a way that allowed me to see just how much life can be different, or that we could live differently and have more peace about our lives. But those seasons prepared me for where I would eventually go later in life.

It's important not to exceed your season or purpose and try to transform it into something else. This can be distracting; if God needs you in a particular place but you're too preoccupied with being elsewhere, you'll miss the purpose and lesson you need to learn for the test to advance to the next level.

There's always a test to get to the next level. That doesn't mean that you're going to have to go through something crazy or something bad to advance. It means that you will be faced with a challenge.

That challenge may not be a challenge for some people, but it could be a significant hurdle for others. However, learning to embrace life, accept ourselves, grow, and understand who we are, where we are, and why we are will help us navigate obstacles.

For people, places, or things, just as some people could be bad for you, something could be bad for you, a place could be bad for you, and staying in your hometown could be bad for you. But leaving that place because that season of your life is over.

A season can represent an age or a portion of your life as it evolves, as your life begins to shift, lessons start to register, and life begins to make sense. You start to grow in knowledge, wisdom, and understanding, moving differently, doing things differently, and thinking about things differently. Consequently, you become different. However, it takes various seasons of your life to learn and perceive different things. Some challenges may not be challenges; they may be opportunities for you to witness something that fosters growth, so that when you face a sure thing, you know how to handle it.

You don't always have to go through something bad to advance. Sometimes, you need to learn from different sources: people, places, experiences, observation, or a book like this. You learn how to see; oh, that's what that is. How do I navigate so I don't make a mistake? Or how do I learn from something I did before so that I'm doing something different when I get to this place?

I'm learning to change the course of my history through my behavior and the things I expose myself to—what I'm willing to grow and learn about—so I am not stuck in this spot or remain stagnant for the rest of my life or for too long, missing a season that I'm supposed to be in. Now, I feel like I'm playing catch-up because I didn't keep up when God was exposing me to the things and different stuff so that I can grow properly.

The exposure you need for growth will take you where you need to go. The things that you're exposed to are the things that will grow you, but you have to know when, where, why, and how to navigate around the distractions.

What is a distraction? It is anything that takes you off your course. Partying too much, going to church too much, smoking weed too much, engaging in hardcore drugs, and struggling to function day to day can all be distractions. The Hold-up Theory aims to identify distractions, learn from your experiences of being distracted, and ensure you never experience that distraction again.

The theories in this book will inspire you and help you grow to a point where what you used to think, what held you back, bound you, and threw you off course, will no longer limit you. It will take you from a place of uncertainty, where you relied on liquor and other distractions to get through life, to a point where you can face life head-on. Recognize the distractions. Identify what is holding you back.

Identify what holds you back, whether it's your mindset, a relationship, a family member, a situation, a job, or a place. Be like the seed planted in the ground. Inside that seed is a husk that breaks open when the seed is placed in the ground and receives the right combination of temperature, heat, and moisture. Once it breaks open, it can take root and be grounded in the soil, allowing it to grow.

Now, some seeds grow upward, and some seeds grow downward. Certain seeds and roots must develop deeply in the soil before they can rise, grow, and become strong. So sometimes, when you're held up, recognize the difference between being held up in what God needs you to experience for growth, versus being held back by a distraction.

God, the creator of all living things, can tell you, "I need you here." I need you here to pray, listen, focus, and see. I need you here so that you can heal. I need you here to identify the issues you must fix before progressing to the next level.

Being held up can mean being stuck in your emotions, not understanding or seeing what's right in front of you, or being unable to embrace something God brings into your life because of past experiences or events. It may also stem from a lack of communication that hinders your growth.

But that brings us back to who you are around. What are you being exposed to? What are they experiencing? Are they healed enough to grow alongside you? Because if you are healed and dealing with someone who isn't, it could slow your progress. However, if they're healing, you can be that friend to help them grow. But if they become a hindrance because you've become a crutch for them, you will be held back; you don't need anyone to pull you down.

You don't need anybody you have to drag because eventually that slows you down and pulls you back from where you're supposed to be, where you're supposed to go, and who you should know. People you are supposed to have been around can be held back by somebody else's lack of communication, respect, ability to see the potential within you, or the inability of you guys to feed each other.

If they are meant to be with you or around you, this is not the time for that due to a lack of ability to grow, a lack of respect, or an inability to nourish each other's souls properly. In that case, it doesn't mean you won't be able to connect later in life unless something unfortunate occurs. If the bridges are burned or God is trying to distance you from people for a specific reason, it will ultimately help you grow; one move made out of season could jeopardize it all. Additionally, if you perceive a situation in an unhealthy manner that hinders growth or is not meant to be, that can lead to accountability issues.

You might come off as unkind if you meet people instead of inviting them in and being friendly. Those individuals could help you heal and grow through experiences such as losing a loved one, losing a job, divorce, or achieving success. Each situation carries its pressures—success brings as much weight as loss. However, if you push away those who could support you, you might be holding yourself back.

However, if you let in the wrong people when you're succeeding, when you're growing, when God has you at his pace and flow, allowing someone into your life could cut off your increase in flow and ability to grow. Finding people for one reason and identifying why they are around you is essential. What's the reason? Is it for a season, or is it for a lifetime?

Do we vibe the same, or are our minds alike in the sense that we share the same goals? We should possess the same mindful, purposeful souls that will allow us to grow and become better individuals, together, and enrich the world. This should be for friends, family, places, and things—whatever you can imagine that might lift you. If social media becomes a hindrance and you're not growing, let it go before it interferes with your path. It may be a season where you must distance yourself from social media or step back from your parents to learn and mature. You may even have to lose people to find yourself. That will not always be the case. God will allow you to grow with people who are successfully growing, but you won't be able to grow with people who are unwilling to grow.

If you surround yourself with people eager to grow, they could become lifelong friends. Some individuals may enter your life for a season and end up having a lifetime presence, while others may come in for a specific reason and become a long-term presence. Sometimes, a person's season in your life can turn into a lifetime. However, letting someone linger in your life without a valid reason for their continued presence may hold you back. It could confuse those who are meant to meet that person when you step aside.

You're supposed to date someone, but they're meant to date someone else to gain specific experiences and exposure to certain situations. However, they are meant to have broken up and moved on, and now they are intended to date you, not cheat. I'm not suggesting otherwise, and if you're cheating, Speaking Freedom does not condone cheating in any way, shape, form, or fashion.

However, suppose two grown, mature adults seek to have extramarital affairs within their relationship. In that case, that is their business and their prerogative, whether they are in a polyamorous relationship or a single monogamous one, whether they enjoy threesomes, foursomes, or don't want to have sex at all.

They want to be together because they love each other, whether it's a nun or someone else. We do not condone cheating, but whatever love is, being integral means you don't have to lie, cheat, or steal to experience it—we support it. If you are happy, if it is purposeful, and if it helps each other grow their souls, we support it. We do not condone cheating.

We do not condone manipulative acts. We do not condone narcissistic behavior. We are here to help you learn, grow, and get unstuck from all those things that either hurt yourself or hurt others or hurt you because you hurt others.

You never know who might be a blessing. It could be an angel in disguise. But if you're lying, cheating, stealing, and acting evilly, or if you're being manipulative, fake, or phony, and not being honorable towards what you say, those behaviors can hinder you. They can hurt the people who are supposed to help you grow, those who can show you things, and those who can nourish you. If you ruin or make toxic relationships that could have lasted a lifetime, it could change how you're aligned with your purpose and alter how you're meant to do things.

The reason is the season's lifetime. Who's around for what reason? Are they there for a particular season, or should they be there for a lifetime? Because you cannot have sex with people who are supposed to be your friends for a lifetime and not expect some drama. Now, if you all are just into freaking stuff and just partying and having sex together, that's one thing. But if you're playing manipulative games with people that are meant to be in your life for long-term reasons, or your lifetime of seasons, and you hurt those who are supposed to help you, or you help those who have hurt you, it can throw off everything that God has planned for you.

You might be afraid to move forward if you get hurt too deeply. If you hurt the wrong person, the individual who was meant to help you progress may be delayed or halted, or God may need to prepare someone else to fulfill a role intended for the person you hurt. You may never find that same individual again. It'll either be better or worse.

I'm not saying that only one person can help you fulfill your purpose. But once you encounter the people you're supposed to have in your life, you have to nurture those relationships and set aside anything that could tarnish or hurt them.

You must ensure that you eliminate any distractions while not attaching your destiny and purpose to anyone. Instead, appreciate everyone you allow into your life, whether they are there for a season, a reason, or a lifetime. However, it is crucial not to cling to those who are meant to be in your life only for a season or a reason. It's vital not to distort the relationship you are meant to have with any person or place.

If you're supposed to be doing something, make sure not to pervert the innocence of your calling. When I say pervert the relationship, I don't necessarily mean nudity and being "nasty"; I mean pervert the relationship in the sense of turning it into something that it's not supposed to be. If you're meant to be a blessing to someone, and that person puts you on drugs, you've turned that relationship into something it was never intended to be. And I'm not talking about smoking weed.

If you are meant to help someone in their career but end up having sex with them, you have transformed that relationship into something it wasn't intended to be. Unless you're both single, open to being together, and believe your purposes align in a way that fosters mutual growth.

In that scenario, you commit to that relationship, and then you engage in sexual activities with others together, instead of cheating. There's a time and place for everything, but you must ensure that you're not being held back or clinging to something that will impede your progress. Are people for a reason, a season, or for a lifetime?

What are red flags?

Start identifying the things that trigger you, upset you, make you angry, anxious, hinder your ability to move forward, or prevent you from progressing as you should. What factors hinder you from being of good service? What barriers hold you back from helping others? What prevents you from believing in yourself and recognizing your beauty? What stops you from being in a relationship? What keeps you from being faithful?

What holds you back from being vulnerable and communicating well with the people around you?

What keeps you from letting go of those who should not be in your life? What prevents you from telling someone you love and need them and want to embrace, be around, and share your world with them? What hinders you from being a good parent? What holds you back, or what triggers your fear? What prompts you to have faith?

Take note of everything that changes your mood, affects how you feel about yourself, how you move forward with God, and how you live out your faith. Don't ignore red flags.

Don't ignore the yellow ones either. Take note of the green lights. Pay attention to when you feel like God is telling you to go. Take notes when you sense something warning you to stop danger, stranger danger, stranger danger. Also, take note of when you feel uncomfortable around someone.

Please note the people who gossip and how it makes you feel. Observe when you start to gossip, and consider why you're discussing that person, especially if it doesn't help them grow or benefit anyone's success concerning the information you're sharing about them.

Good, bad, or indifferent — what does this mean for you? Are you establishing meaningful goals or learning from the experiences you encounter?

Gossip continues to be gossip when the intent is to belittle someone or when there's nothing else to discuss. However, if you express, "oh my God, did you see what happened with such and such and such and such?" because you can relate, it reflects your learning process, your observations, or how the situation has influenced your growth, ultimately helping you to evolve into a better version of yourself.

Please do not compare yourself to people going through something, because at some point, everyone endures challenges, whether it's growth, sickness, or financial hardship. No matter your financial tax bracket or level, there is always something to learn and grow from. A financial situation will always stress you or cause you to think deeply about your next steps. It doesn't matter if you're a millionaire, a thousandaire, busted, broke, or significantly in debt.

Everybody has bills; typically, the more you earn, the higher your bills. Normally, the more you earn, the more you spend. So don't ever think for a second that just because someone else has money or possesses certain things, they don't experience challenges, endure difficulties, or have to learn from struggles. Even a billionaire might sometimes run low on resources or face delays in accessing their funds. If all their money is in the bank, guess what? They may still need to wait for transactions to be approved, authorized, or accepted.

Just because you have an 800 credit score or a million dollars in the bank doesn't mean everything you try to buy will come easily. It doesn't guarantee the absence of roadblocks, distractions, or experiences that provide valuable lessons. Having money does not eliminate every problem.

It might create some. The goal is to determine what constitutes a distraction. Is making money a distraction? It can be if you don't know how to use it wisely. If you become so focused on earning that you think, "Oh, I've got to do this, I've got to get this money," then that money may begin to control you.

That money can become more important than your family and friends. It will become more important than your health. It will become the most important thing to you. And then all you will have is some wealth or riches because if you're not whole and everything is not going right, that's not well. You have a lot of money, but you are not wealthy if you're unhappy.

If you're not growing, I don't believe you're wealthy because if you just got money, anybody can be rich and miserable. Don't be rich and miserable. Be wealthy, be whole, be complete.

But you must know what distracts you, what holds you up, and what is a roadblock. What triggers growth or stagnation? How do you see yourself progressing based on your environment, circumstances, current knowledge, current goals, and the growth that you expect for yourself alone? It's good to have people around.

It's unhealthy to rely on people as crutches, preventing you from becoming independent and self-sufficient. It's essential to avoid always needing help, advice, handouts, rides, or places to stay. Instead of consistently asking others to do things for you that you aren't willing to do for yourself, focus on learning and growing so you can do more.

It is essential. You must learn who you are, why you are, and what you are. What do I mean by what you are? What's your heritage? What's your history? Sometimes, what blocks you or hinders your progress are your beliefs based on the reasons behind them, the traditions you cling to simply because your grandmother told you to, without knowing their origins.

When dealing with people, are their characteristics compatible with who you are and your values? Now, we're not talking about what a person's sexual preference is or whether they do this or that.

Do their core values reflect what you value? Do their characteristics align with what is apparent? People can have core values that do not represent how they act and behave. They can know a lot, but that doesn't mean they're applying everything they know. How is this important to you? Because you could be that person.

You could be holding up somebody else, or somebody else could be holding you up. But the chapter we're in helps you understand how to recognize what holds you back from your success and goals and how to put people, things, and places in their proper place. Just because you grew up there doesn't mean you must stay there.

Just because someone helped you learn something doesn't mean they are supposed to be in your life for the rest of your life. Your teachers don't stay in your life forever. What if every person you met was a teacher, and some are lifelong teachers, and some are teachers that you just needed to help you learn that lesson to get you where you needed to go long term?

If you consider everyone in life a teacher, you can learn from every situation. If you can learn from every situation, you're less likely to be held up by a distraction because you know that you're learning a lesson, and once you learn that lesson and apply what you learned, you will advance. The education system shows you the importance of teachers, leaders, and someone to guide you.

The question is, where did they get the concept from? Did they get it from ancient Egypt? Did they get it from an African tribe? Did they learn about gentrification from the ancients? Did historians take what they learned from ancient times and turn it into what they needed to rule nations? Did they go and possess land where they didn't belong? Did they go and possess beliefs and turn them into religion?

How can your belief system support you if you don't know what you believe, not just what you believe, but why? Do you know why you believe what you believe? Why is that more important than the belief? Understanding why you believe what you believe can prepare you for what you're designed to endure.

You'll break if what you believe isn't backed by a good reason for your belief. You'll stop. Your beliefs will hold you back because you don't even know why you hold them. Your religion. Why do you believe it? Why did your granny believe it? Who helped them learn about the way you view religion? We're not talking about a relationship with God, but religion itself.

Let's consider Spiritual Human Behavior and how all things work together. Each religion can teach one another something, so the world can love better, become one, harmonize, and grow from what we know.

Most of the time, we are held back by the degree of separation that stems from how we believe in our creator. You must have the mindset to apply, adjust, and adapt to everything you're learning about yourself, the people around you, and your interests.

Learning what's unappealing to you is more important than learning what you love. If you learn what you don't like, you understand what's unacceptable. What are you not willing to accept, what are you unwilling to do, and what will you avoid?

These become the red flags. One of the final pieces of understanding a holdup involves knowing how to navigate around it. It comes from learning from previous experiences, observation, and observing the people around you. So if you see something you dislike about another person, learn not to create that same outcome by changing your thoughts. Shift your mindset and how you apply what you're learning about yourself and your thought process, and consider who influenced the way you began to think and how others are influencing you.

It may not be something they said or did. It might come from what you witnessed, the actions you learned, or their absence, leading you to appreciate the unique things they had to offer. Yet, your mindset must focus on growth, and be willing to review and reflect on your experiences so you can learn from them.

Section 3
Expectation of Self & Others

Section 3 Introduction: Call Your Bluff Theory

The Call Your Bluff Theory is what you do to ensure that you are getting the results that you desire, whether it is calling your bluff with yourself or calling your bluff with the people around you. So, what is a bluff, and why would you like to call it? A bluff is when people offer a lot, say a lot, and act like they want to do everything. However, not everyone is willing to follow through.

This doesn't have to be about a job, a person, a thing, or a place. It's about ensuring that when you say you're going to do something, you do it, rather than just talking for the sake of talking. When people offer you things, present opportunities, or act as if they want to do something or work with you, are you truly committed, or is it talk? Because I'm going to call the bluff. I'm going to see if you're going to do what you say you're going to do, or if you're going to forget what you said and run around corners, shuffling and avoiding talking about what you offered or what you committed to for yourself or others.

You'll frequently use this to ensure results and hold those around you accountable, just as you hold yourself accountable. So, how does calling your bluff assist? If you meet individuals who sell empty promises or mislead you, pretending to take action when they're not, they might say things like, "We're going to do this, we're going to work, we're going to make this happen."

See who's really about that life versus who's just talking like they're about that life. I don't care if you're dating or somebody says, "I got a job for you." See if they really have a job for you or if they are offering empty promises.

When somebody says, "Call me whenever you need it, I'll help you no matter what," call them and see if they help you. If you need it, no matter what, because nine times out of ten, you'll get one of two results. Either they are going to live up to what they said, or they're not going to live up to what they said, and now you know how to deal with them moving forward.

This is one of the most essential theories or methods in this theory book because it's the method you will use to test each theory within yourself and with the people around you. So you have to ensure as much as possible that you are willing to go to the next level of whatever the bluff is, because if somebody is offering you something that you really aren't sure you want to do, then that's not a bluff you call. You call the bluff based on what you are really willing to do.

What can people expect from you? If you say I will do such a thing, it doesn't have to be a specific time, but will you actually do it? Will you hold yourself to your own words?

Is your word your bond? Ensuring that what is presented is precisely as it should be is what you call the "call your bluff" method. I'm presenting this to you, but it's this; you know, like many people who say, "Yeah, I've got you no matter what. We're good, we're good, we're family," but if something happens and you need them, they're nowhere to be found. Now that's blood, business, friendship, platonic, romantic, whatever the case.

The "call your bluff" theory, especially when giving an ultimatum, is the most effective way to assess your relationship with someone because one of two things will happen. You will either grow or have the chance to let go of something that is not real. We hope you use this method to test every theory in this book, rather than the book itself, as it is intended to be self-explanatory. It contains a variety of methods and theories you can utilize to enhance your thought process, enabling your growth in ways you haven't experienced before, based on case studies, research, and more.

Now, let's discuss calling your bluff. How will it help you evaluate yourself? Calling your bluff will ensure that you truly understand what you claim to represent. If you tell someone, "okay, if you come and approach me like this, then I'm going to do this," or "if you present this, then I'm going to move forward and do this," are you really prepared to follow through with what you're saying, or are you just talking nonsense?

The goal and purpose of the call-your-bluff theory and method is to ensure accountability, that your word is your bond, and that whatever you say, you do. Whatever you speak is something you want to come true, and you're not just blowing smoke. Now, your word is unreliable, and nobody trusts you.

It's essential to ensure that your word is trustworthy and that people can rely on your words. Can others have confidence in your dependability? Nobody wants an unreliable person around them. You become a liability, merely there to mooch and see how much you can get—leeching and taking without any intention of contributing or helping others grow.

This involves both self-evaluation and evaluating the people around you. Once people realize that they cannot just tell you anything, you'll recognize lies, which will free you from having to engage with fake, phony, and fraudulent individuals that come and go. Most people can't handle the pressure of the call your bluff theory because it tells you who they really are. Let people talk.

Let people tell you whatever. See what they do. Please put them in a position to act on their stated desires without you having to beg, ask, plead, or make any dramatic efforts to encourage them to do what they have already expressed wanting to do. Anyone who truly wishes to accomplish something will do it.

They won't make excuses for anything in any way, shape, or form. The call your bluff method is not an ultimatum. It is testing the spirit by the spirit.

Holding that person accountable for what they're supposed to be doing. So, how do you call their bluff? You call a person's bluff by holding them to their word. If a guy says he wants to date you, tell him you're interested.

If he doesn't date you, then he was talking. If your boss says they would like to give you a promotion, they open a position, you apply for the job, and you do everything you're supposed to do. If you don't get it, then they were talking.

If someone says they want to do something nice for you, but you have to beg them to do it, they are just talking. They will find a way to do anything they want for you in real life. They will not leave you on a wild goose chase. They are not going to make you feel any way. You call their bluff. You make them accountable for whatever it is they said.

Make them acknowledge what they said and ensure you know what you will do if the bluff is called or they fold. You're either going to rise or fold each time with every method as you go through the theories, especially the upcoming ones. As you continue to explore the remaining theories, you will realize how crucial calling your bluff is, particularly when dealing with people.

So it will be for self-evaluation and to keep everything around you in check. What are you really about? What do you desire? How do you envision yourself growing and inspiring those around you? Are you a person of your word? Ensure you always position yourself to pursue what's next while being content and maintaining your current focus as you develop. Calling a person's bluff is about ensuring that things are what they appear to be.

That you reach the level you need to be at, and that whoever is claiming they will do whatever is genuinely about doing whatever. You don't have to call every single bluff. You don't have to test everything unless that's your chosen path. Don't test things for which you're not interested in the outcome. However, know that calling a person's bluff will reveal exactly where you stand with them and where they stand with you. It's not like the boy who cried wolf, and you're just taking action for the sake of it.

This is serious. This is how you're going to keep your soul in check. Like I said, it's testing the spirit by the spirit.

If you say that you're about this type of purpose or that you're this way, okay, well, let's see you be that way all the time. And not that you have to be a certain way, but whatever you say, let that be what it is. You'll then see how you can use this to help you grow. So the goal is to either elevate or reevaluate. Now that you've called the bluff, are we going further, or do we need to figure out what's happening?

Am I experiencing growth, or do I need to reevaluate how I'm approaching what I say I'm trying to do? Am I taking the steps and following the procedures that will truly get me there? This is me calling my own bluff.

This means holding yourself accountable, not just to those around you. Are you doing what you claim you will do based on necessity, rather than foolishness, or acquiring unnecessary things? Are you acting with intention that aligns with your purpose? Are you making yourself open to what leads to your purpose?

Are the people around you engaging in actions that lead them to their purpose, and that will enable you to achieve your purpose? They don't have to be connected; everyone needs to be purpose-minded. Ensure you're calling their bluff, not on matters primarily concerning you, but regarding their pursuit of what they truly want to do.

Calling your bluff involves holding yourself and those around you accountable. As I mentioned, you are responsible for your words, your actions, and all the effort you invest in everything you do. Once the bluff is called, you position yourself to reach your highest potential.

You can place yourself where you want to go because you've removed distractions not meant for you. It's essential to recognize that calling your bluff isn't solely about highlighting others but also about identifying within yourself where you're inclined to stop and where your bluff lies.

What boundaries will you not cross, or what destinations do you want to avoid? Calling your bluff is a crucial tool to help you advance in life with the right people, as you need individuals who keep their word. It's your most significant asset outside your talent, gift, and skill.

We will also introduce some new factors that will influence how you deal with people, how to manage them, and what you should genuinely expect from them.

Integrity Factor

The first factor is the Integrity Factor. The integrity factor refers to the degree of integrity you maintain throughout the peaks and valleys of your career and life, ensuring that you uphold your principles as events unfold. Therefore, if you become incredibly famous and gain access and the ability to do anything you wish with anyone, do not use that as an opportunity to compromise your integrity. Here are actions that can tarnish your integrity.

Deceiving others, exploiting individuals, drugging and engaging with people, committing rape, and taking advantage of others.

When you factor in integrity, it will indicate how long and far your career can go, how your acknowledgments and achievements will last beyond your career, and the height of your career. This factor became particularly relevant after witnessing a highly esteemed actor go through situations that questioned his absolute integrity, which ultimately detracted from many of his accomplishments due to various instances where he did not demonstrate integrity.

Unfortunately, many people lack integrity by misleading, manipulating, cheating, scheming, and treating others poorly, and these actions often go unnoticed. For many, such behaviors seem to be within their control, and they have permitted them to persist in their lives.

Karma Factor

Karma is another factor. The karma factor plays over the integrity factor because you can do everything you want, including conniving, cheating, stealing, misusing people, and just doing all types of things. The integrity factor will come into play when it's time for karma to meet its date, and karma is when you are faced with issues that lack integrity. Karma is not always bad.

If you did great things, guess what your karma factor will be: inducive and inclusive of great things. If you mistreat people and do bad things, then your karma will come in two different ways. It will come by way of something being done, something that happens, or something in a physical sense.

However, the other flip side of karma is the guilt, shame, and mental torture that you put yourself through by doing someone wrong. Then you always think, "Oh my god, that's going to come back on me because I did this, I said this, or I treated someone like this." Karma is not when somebody viciously or maliciously does something bad to you.

Karma is a natural happening. Karma means I don't have to cut you because you cut me. Karma defeats the need for me to do anything towards anyone because karma will play itself out.

Whatever goes around comes around, so whatever bad you've done will return. If you cheated and lied to someone or tricked them into a situation, their karma may involve dealing with the issues, drama, and feelings it has brought them to. However, your karma will stem from your actions to harm others, manipulate others, and make them feel a certain way.

Karma hinges on the integrity factor, which influences how you act when you might do something frowned upon. Have enough integrity to do the right thing simply because it's right, not because you fear it might come back on you. When you do the right thing for the right reasons, your integrity remains strong, and you won't have to worry about anything coming back on you for any reason.

Even if you do it just because you know that karma will come back around, having integrity will take you much farther than being talented, witty, or having a presence or a career height that reaches beyond what you've ever imagined. Integrity will keep your standards. Integrity will hold on to your accomplishments.

Integrity will keep you in the will and divine purpose that you are designed to be in. The next factor is the power factor, a matter of utilizing your power for the right things. It goes along with the integrity factor because your integrity comes back to you, and anything that you do without integrity can lead you to a place where everything you've ever worked on can be snatched away from you.

The Power Factor

The power factor is understanding your power and how to use it. Many people manipulate their power, using it to hold it over others, get their way, satisfy their desires, and exploit those around them.

When you wield power incorrectly, it weakens due to a loss of integrity. As your power diminishes, its effectiveness declines. It's comparable to needing one hundred and fifty volts of power. If you misuse your power in ways that negatively impact your reputation, you'll find yourself with only one hundred and twenty volts instead of the one hundred and fifty you need. Actions that do not align with integrity will compromise your power in other areas.

The Money Factor

The money factor is the ability to finance whatever you desire. However, being able to finance what you can does not erase the fact that you must have integrity. You need to know how to use your power in ways that help and empower others.

If you use your power to belittle, disarm, or harm people, then your power becomes mute and void. However, you create an unstoppable force by combining integrity, power, and money. You will become unstoppable by using your power with integrity and your money to support your actions grounded in integrity.

However, if you use your money to manipulate people, lord over them, or misuse them, your money will lose value. Money can buy almost anything. However, money will not buy you integrity.

Money will not buy you peace. Money will not buy you happiness. Money can buy products.

It can buy material things. And yes, you may be able to go and be sad with more money, but money will not fix your sadness. The money factor is knowing how to use your money to empower the people surrounding you, without lording over them.

The Fame Factor

The last factor is fame. Once you blow up, you will have to endure a whole different undertaking. There will be much more criticism, judgment, and an all-eyes-on-me feeling because now you have fame.

Fame is not for the weak; it is not for the weary, and it can tarnish, harm, or manipulate your judgment regarding how you deal with people, handle responsibilities, make decisions with integrity, use your power, manage your money, and maintain your fame. Fame is something that people toy with. Anybody can be famous.

Currently, someone who has disabilities, is mentally challenged, or is too young to handle fame can become famous. Fame is subjective. I do not belittle anyone who is disabled or mentally challenged for becoming famous, but what we often overlook is that, most of the time, these individuals are famous not for accomplishing something significant, but because they are being mocked, laughed at, and joked about, resulting in their fame.

Fame is a monster that requires a lot of time and attention, and is something you cannot run from. Once you are famous and known, you can not be unknown. Even if you hide out or stay away, somebody will know you for your fame.

The fame factor is very important because you must know how to manage fame; it can manipulate your integrity and your identity, and can begin to alter your character.

You must always remain true to yourself, regardless of what you possess—integrity, power, money, or fame. This is why it's essential to explore these theories. Understand who you are, why you are, where you are, and how you arrived at this point, so your integrity is never questioned.

For your power to be as strong as possible, and for your money to not only belong but also empower people. It helps build the community and does great things other than buying stuff. Now, with the fame factor, again, each is their own.

However, be aware of who you become when you become famous. Money, power, and fame only amplify who you are at your core. If you're not a good person when you're broke, you're not going to be a better person when you're famous, have money, or have power.

If you are a good person because you're broke, when you become famous, have money or power, then whoever you are on the inside, for real, will show up. If you're a good person, then the good things will show up and manifest. If you're a bad person, those bad things and those qualities will again manifest.

Many of these aspects also relate to who you're connected with. If you're connected with positive individuals, they'll bring out the best in you. However, if you're surrounded by negative people—those who are sour, bitter, or upset—they may help you manifest your desires. Still, they will also influence what manifests within and around them, because you are not stronger than your environment.

Either your environment changes you, or you end up changing your environment.

Chapter 6: The Band-Aid Effect

The Band-Aid Effect is the theory that allows us to discuss what we do when we want to avoid healing or examining our wounds. The theory also has different levels and layers of how band-aids are used. Instead of addressing the dilemmas of your life, you do things to cover them so you don't have to process how you truly feel. This is often done when emotions are shamed, making the person numb to most emotions outside of anger.

This particular theory has many compartments because of different types of band-aids, emotional band-aids, material band-aids, and many external band-aids that people use to avoid internal dilemmas. This theory helps us describe some possible band-aids you may need to remove.

The Band-Aid Effect is a defense mechanism that does not address feelings that must be confronted and cared for. Addressing your internal conflicts can help you breathe and heal rather than just covering them up with something.

When you cover things for too long, you worsen whatever it is because it needs oxygen to breathe. Not addressing it means you're not allowing it to get air. To breathe, you must uncover and allow it to be exposed to receive what it needs from the oxygen and air that help it dry and heal itself.

Like any bandage, if you leave it on too long, it can worsen. It can also cause an infection if it doesn't receive enough air for the skin to heal and dry. I encourage you to be very open-minded when I begin discussing the different aspects of the Band-Aid Effect.

The top band-aid effects are the defense mechanisms people employ to protect themselves and avoid vulnerability and healing. Sometimes, individuals are unaware that they are evading healing. Occasionally, they opt for what feels good in the moment instead of seeking what might provide lasting satisfaction. Until you are willing and able to do that, you will remain in a state of unfulfillment.

When experiencing a band-aid effect, you often feel a void or a sense of wholeness. However, unaddressed issues hinder you from recognizing your wholeness at its full potential, preventing you from assessing your soul's growth. This blockage keeps you from developing and embracing your soul purpose, allowing you to walk in a way that leads to complete fulfillment, happiness, and alignment with your true path. Let's begin with the portion on defense mechanisms.

Defense Mechanisms

The *defense mechanism* aspect of the band-aid effect includes behaviors such as avoiding confrontations or pushing people away. The pushing away aspect is particularly noteworthy because there are different phases of getting to know others. During this process, individuals sometimes get hurt.

People may have experiences that influence them; I don't want to say baggage, as suggesting they carry it with them may not be accurate. However, they recognize how different situations transformed them, how they caused pain, and what lessons they learned. Thus, any indication of what they have overcome may lead them to turn away, revert to the previous situation, or seek further clarity before proceeding.

Pushing someone away is never beneficial, but it arises from an unresolved issue within the individual. There's a difference between pushing someone away and being uninterested in them, lacking a desire to grow together, and acknowledging the endpoint. None of this is pushing someone away, but setting a boundary and preference for how you want to structure your life.

What it means to push people away is that they have everything in the right area, are focused on the right things, and are willing to come together and build with you based on solid terms, and then you clam up and push them away. In contrast, if you've been through something and learned a lesson from it, you need to reflect on everything you didn't like about the outcome to progress as intended. Doing that is like taking off the band-aid.

You must address the issue to grow from situations where you have determined the outcome wasn't favorable or needed adjustments. Identify the problem, and figure out how to avoid making this particular decision again if it arises. Sometimes, this may involve saying no to people you would have previously said yes to, or even saying no to people you have said yes to. It's crucial to avoid compromising in this area to prevent being caught in the same situation you're trying to avoid.

You must always understand there is a variation between what is and what could be. The paradox theory will partially cover this, but it is relevant and needs addressing. In the band-aid theory, we recognize that many people have been hurt and don't know how to navigate the terrain.

Instead of addressing their various areas of pain, they often find ways to combat it. Those who were broke growing up resorted to manipulative behavior and lying to deal with that. Some people weren't allowed to do certain things, leading them to be more deceitful than someone with the freedom to act as they wished.

The band-aid is that you tell lies instead of being honest and truthful. Instead of going out and earning your wages, you manipulate people or scam people to get your way, but you're never learning to face whatever makes you feel that something will not work for you, so you seek the easy way.

What you don't want to do is sell yourself short. You don't want to take the easy way out. It's beneficial to use ointment on a cut, and it's helpful to use band-aids, but eventually, you have to let the moisture within that wound dry up to heal.

If it stays moist, it will not heal. It will remain an active, hurting scar—not even a scar; it will be a wound, and then you might get infected because of the constant moisture.

Anything can happen if you layer things on top of each other. If you are hurting, don't allow one person to diminish your view of everyone by thinking, 'This one person did this to me, so now I'm going to treat all people this way based on what someone else did or didn't do.' Even when men discuss relationships or building bonds, personality traits, and the differences between males and females, they often want to portray the male as the dog.

He's the person who's constantly manipulating or always cheating or always acting like this towards women. It's commonly seen that men are the only source of immaturity, that almost all men are immature and don't know how to love a woman, or things like that.

Society doesn't give men credit for encountering women who are manipulators, incapable of loving properly, unsupportive, unfaithful, or unable to obtain a job or contribute meaningfully. There are many factors at play when it comes to womanizers or manipulative women.

Consider gold diggers. Gold digging is another form of a band-aid, and the reason it is considered a band-aid is that when you decide to use men or exchange your body for financial gain, you are placing yourself at the lowest end of the totem pole, often not learning anything that would improve your situation.

If he decides he no longer wants you and finds someone new, you'll move on to the next person who meets that need, without addressing your own. This means your lifestyle is always at risk of changing. The aim of recognizing this is to encourage you to heal, grow, and provide the lifestyle you desire for yourself, so it's not at the mercy of someone who might wake up and not want you anymore. (Men are Gold Diggers too, so this is not women exclusive.)

Why did you start relying on men for financial support? Why did you choose this as your main option? While in that situation, are you making wise decisions with the money you receive? There are two sides to this matter, and I plan to incorporate the paradox theory because it's like comparing gold to gold-plated items. It's crucial to discern what is genuine versus what appears genuine, understanding the difference between your true desires and something that only seems to fulfill them but ultimately falls short.

The paradox theory involves recognizing the distinction between deceptive illusions and reality. This chapter assists you in pinpointing the aspects you use to mask your insecurities. While not everyone experiences insecurity, if you're reading this book, there are likely areas in your life that you wish to enhance. Additionally, there are people in your life you want to see grow, which necessitates addressing both community-wide and personal insecurities that hinder our spiritual and emotional growth.

Repression

One of the first defense mechanisms is *repression*, similar to avoidance. With repression, you mentally and often unconsciously block out uncomfortable emotions. In contrast, with avoidance, if you can avoid dealing with something, you will do so rather than confront the thing that has hurt you.

People tend to believe that if you forget it, you can't be hurt. If you don't address it by avoidance, and do everything not to think about it, it gives the impression that you can't be hurt. But what we fail to realize or understand sometimes is that avoidance and repression do not heal you as much as they cause you to have to face that challenge over and over again. It's also important to note that most people who are diagnosed with memory issues, especially dementia, are often "haunted" by and struggle with handling otherwise suppressed memories.

The more you repress things, the more they resurface when something reminds you of that issue. Each time that issue comes up, it gets repressed instead of being addressed directly, preventing you from discovering how to heal yourself in that area. For the most part, repression is simply a classic form of avoidance, a mental evasion of a problem.

Defense mechanisms can lead to a wide array of behaviors. This is where you find shopaholics, workaholics, and possibly users and abusers, as well as drug addicts. Repression is not the only defense mechanism that causes people to employ superficial solutions; these areas also lead individuals to apply quick fixes.

A defense mechanism is one sort of bandage, but there are different types of Band-Aids.

It's a band-aid when you shop because you don't want to feel. That's not just shopping for enjoyment; it's not shopping for a need, and it's not shopping because of anything other than to avoid feeling bad. Addressing things that make you feel bad should cause these questions to run through your mind.

What are you reminded of that makes you feel this way? Sometimes, we shouldn't feel anything about anything because nothing connects us to it directly. When you are connected to it directly, something internal has likely been repressed and covered up so that it cannot be addressed. The goal now is to figure out how to deal with those repressed thoughts, and that's where spiritual human behavior comes in.

To address those repressed thoughts, you must identify their underlying causes. What motivates you to suppress them rather than confront them? They may stem from childhood trauma, interpersonal relationship issues, workplace stress, or feelings of self-doubt and lack of support. Repression typically occurs with more serious issues, such as if someone has experienced rape, molestation and other forms of violence.

If someone has been robbed, if someone has experienced extreme trauma, then repression and avoidance are the two most commonly used defense mechanisms. I know, especially as a veteran, many veterans who have PTSD avoid thinking about having PTSD.

They never address their feelings; sometimes, not addressing one's feelings can worsen the situation. It can deepen emotions, erode self-confidence, and trigger agitation when something brings forth those repressed feelings.

Projection

The next defense mechanism that we will discuss is *projection*.

Projection is more dramatic because it involves projecting your feelings, situation, outcome, and outlook onto them. We must consider projection from both the giver and the receiver, as we frequently find situations where someone has experienced something that caused them hurt, pain, or some stressful trauma.

Many people have gone through experiences that caused them pain or trauma. Instead of addressing their issues with a particular situation, they choose to project their anger, fear, uncertainty, grief, and frustration onto others regarding their circumstances.

Now, it's not bad when someone projects onto you because what they're expressing is that they're hurt. They have gone through something that was not good for them. Instead of allowing you to have your moment and individualized experience, they try to project their fears, hatred, and negative feelings onto you. Projection can also take a different direction. It can occur when you've experienced something, and instead of permitting someone else to follow their path regarding that experience, you try to take control.

There is nothing wrong with helping someone assess a situation based on your experience because you've been there. Still, projection is when you erase the possibilities for this person, negating and neglecting their experience and how their situation may differ by imposing what you believe has to come from that situation. There are no options besides what is projected onto you, and people primarily project their fears, anger, and confusion, unless they know and have experienced something. Some factual matters are not determined by your course, path, and experience compared to theirs.

Projection helps you grow by allowing you to see what others have experienced, by using that projection to navigate your own experiences will not always be productive.

Loving, trusting, and respecting someone can be challenging. They may project their fears onto you, limiting your potential and what God can achieve through you and your growth, and they are often quick to judge. Sometimes, those who project do not have their own lives in order, so ensuring that no one is projecting onto you is essential. However, you must also be cautious not to project your fears onto others, as projection is not a form of protection. Unlike rejection, which can provide guidance, projection does not serve the same purpose. Projection is someone else's experience overruling your possibilities.

Another form of projection is not accepting blame. Suppose you are dealing with something and having trouble embracing it. In that case, projection can also suggest that someone else is causing things to happen to you, rather than you reflecting and acknowledging your role in the situation. If I have a thought process that prevents me from accepting how this mindset has developed, it's easier to say I don't have a problem; they have issues with how they view things or present themselves.

Suppose I say I have an issue involving people rather than accepting my responsibility. In that case, I project all the blame onto someone else and act irresponsibly because I cannot acknowledge my part in whatever is happening.

Displacement

The next defense mechanism is *displacement*, where we unjustly mistreat someone because we have been mistreated ourselves. If we're treated poorly at work, the grocery store, or by someone we've interacted with, we may go home and unfairly take it out on someone we love, even though they have done nothing wrong.

This results from displacing our feelings and is almost a form of projection, as we direct our anger and emotions toward someone who is not the source of those feelings. It's similar to going to work, having your boss do something wrong, and then returning home upset. Instead of addressing the situation at work, you might snap at your children, even though they haven't done anything wrong.

We must ensure that when we have an issue, we address it with the individuals involved. If that's impossible or not in your best interest, then you need to reflect on the matter within yourself. We are often compelled to forgive people who aren't necessarily remorseful. Admittedly, sometimes people aren't sorry because they are unaware of their wrongdoing.

They don't recognize the errors you perceive as wrong in their behavior. Sometimes it's simply due to differing opinions. Therefore, when the opportunity arises, you may need to address issues within yourself, regardless of whether you can confront that person, whether they are alive, have moved on, or whatever the circumstances.

It's not always healthy to reintroduce ourselves to situations that hurt or harmed us or from which we haven't fully processed and moved on. We must address the issue within ourselves and figure out why this person did, said, or suggested something that hurt us. You don't have to confront the person to understand why it hurt you. If you can comprehend why something hurt you, avoiding directing that anger at someone who didn't cause that hostility is easier.

You must begin to understand what angers you when you get angry and make sure that you address those things so that you do not take that out on somebody who does not deserve to be treated poorly because somebody treated you poorly. It's about karma in this area and sowing the seeds that you would like to receive. Just because somebody mistreats you doesn't mean you mistreat the next person.

You must maintain that balance of knowing how to transform somebody else's issues, turn anger into power, and convert fear into strength. Make those things into powerful moments so that they don't hang over your head or lord over you like a band-aid. Again, if you leave a band-aid on too long, the skin doesn't have time to dry. If it doesn't dry, the skin can't grow back, regenerating as if it never happened. You might get a little scar, but if you expose it to the necessary elements, it will be less.

Rationalization

The next defense mechanism is *rationalization*. This is where people make excuses for issues we do not want to face.

Instead of saying, "Okay, I have this problem," we excuse our problem. If you're in a relationship and continue to be hurt by someone, instead of saying, "Okay, I know this is what's hurting me," let's figure out how to make it work or call it quits. You rationalize why something is hurting you or why you are doing this.

You try to make an excuse for behavior when, most of the time, there are no excuses. You're simply painting someone differently than what they're showing you their color to be. It's easy to forgive. Forgiveness is great.

We should avoid letting forgiveness lead to a state where we continuously excuse poor treatment from others or ourselves. When we make excuses, we hinder our healing and permit ongoing harm. If someone continues pushing our boundaries, the situation will likely escalate.

It's not going to heal. So this defense mechanism is a Band-Aid because you're making excuses, and the excuse is a Band-Aid. Rationalizing what is happening to you so that you don't have to address the issue is a Band-Aid.

It's okay to understand the reasons, the facts, and the truth, but never make an excuse for why somebody is treating you poorly or why you won't address the issues you know you need to heal and grow.

Denial

The next defense mechanism is *denial,* probably one of the most used.

Let's also discuss *"Christian Denial,"* a term that describes Christians who use religion and God as a Band-Aid or a scapegoat instead of growing and healing themselves. Often, especially for those deeply involved in church or highly religious, they use God and Jesus to deny what is happening in their lives in real time. Instead of addressing an issue or admitting they have a problem, they say

Jesus will fix it without putting in the necessary effort.

Church can be a crutch and a Band-Aid that prevents people from truly healing or growing because they expect a magical experience where God will heal them, help them grow, and guide them on what to do. In reality, the best way to heal is to acknowledge that something needs to be healed, rather than taking it to the altar and acting as if it never existed. Yes, you want to reach a point where its existence no longer bothers you, but you cannot simply wash things away and pretend they never influenced your life or perspective.

How you became who you are today ties into your past. Everything is connected. It's crucial to understand denial, which is acting as if there's no problem when a clear issue exists.

Instead of addressing the problem, people look the other way to deny it—alcoholism is a prime example, as alcoholics often refuse to acknowledge they have a problem, worsening the situation. Rather than admitting, "I do this too much," whether it's alcohol, drugs, church, work, or whatever, you cover it up with a Band-Aid like someone who's been hurt before.

Gold Digger (mindset)

One Band-Aid that is not mental is the gold digger aspect of living. That's where you always look for somebody to pay your bills and take care of you, so you don't have to learn anything. *The Gold Digger mindset is not exclusive to women; plenty of men seek to be taken care of with little effort.

Instead of saying that they've become gold diggers because they don't want to allow people into their lives and their hearts, having been hurt before, people deny that anything is wrong. Some individuals are simply lazy and don't understand what a work ethic is or what it means to earn one's way.

They claim they want to date in exchange for money. While some seek relationships for access to wealth, people often become gold diggers because they're not confronting a deeper issue. You don't have to work necessarily; you don't have to do anything but be at that person's beck and call for when they want to pay you or when they want to do something for you. The gold digger theory is a form of denial because it prevents you from accessing love deeper than financial support. Some gold diggers are raised this way due to poverty and struggle.

This is not necessarily due to hurt. Some gold diggers become gold diggers because they were raised with and taught gold digger ways. Their parents, perhaps their mother, experienced hurt, and instead of teaching their daughter to choose better, they say, "Just go after who's going to give you the most money." That becomes the way of life for this person.

Most gold diggers live lavish lives, but at the end of the day, some are hurting inside because they won't let people in close enough to love them to the depth that they can be loved. When you become a gold digger, there's a significant loss of control because that person is holding that opportunity over your head.

Instead of merely confronting yourself, focusing on your purpose, and recognizing your worth beyond physical beauty or attributes like curves or a flattering figure, learning these truths is essential to avoid the pitfalls of being a gold digger. Every woman with something to offer should seek a man with ambition or resources. Otherwise, if he brings nothing to the table, he might lead you to lose what you already have. If he lacks the knowledge to sustain your achievements, he possesses none of his own.

If discussed, it involves refusing to acknowledge our problems, masking them with other distractions, and denying that there is an issue that needs to be addressed. For example, if you're hurt, avoiding the fact that someone hurts you doesn't change the reality of your pain. It limits your ability to heal and allows that hurt to affect you forever.

That's the one thing, the biggest frustration I have about church and the way they teach people not to address their issues, but to believe God will miraculously change them without addressing the things that control them internally, allowing them to mature in all areas of their lives spiritually. This is the basis of spiritual human behavior. The most significant aspect of denial is denying that you have a specific pattern that causes this particular result and that this result is based on the pattern of your thinking, living, spending, the company you keep, and the environment in which your pattern exists.

All of these factors make a difference when discussing denial.

Regression

The next defense mechanism we will discuss is regression. This occurs when you revert to doing old things that feel more comfortable or make you happier, rather than trying to change.

Whether you like the result or want to do those things to avoid growth and maturity and having to address those issues, it's easier to regress. And regression does not always mean being childish. If you start a new pattern in your life and it gets hard, you can regress to just doing something you used to do that made life easier.

Although you may see results when you begin exercising, it might hurt you unexpectedly. As a result, you might regress to doing less exercise to avoid the pain you have started to feel.

Thus, regression even happens in your thoughts. Suppose you started to think more positively because you were having very negative thoughts. To regress means to stop thinking positively and revert to how you were thinking before attempting to think positively. If you tend to be a pessimist, someone who is always negative, and you begin a new path—let's say you want to think positively now—you wish to adopt a positive mindset.

The initial response often involves regression when facing a trial for the first time. If you aim to remain positive, you won't argue about it. But when someone comes at you, it becomes a test. During this test, you might regress to a state where you lose control. Recognizing that regression is normal can help you learn to progress rather than retreat. Rather than reverting to what's comfortable, what pleases others, or what feels good, especially if you're doing so to avoid personal growth challenges, you may find yourself repressing your true potential.

We don't want you to repress, regress, or return to the same things you hoped to change.

Intellectualization

Intellectualization is where you try to *intellectualize* the result that you receive.

Instead of changing your pattern to get a different result, you try to make an excuse or intellectualize, explaining away why things happened. Still, you have to make specific changes. So let's say you date a particular type of person. Instead of saying, maybe this type of person is unhealthy for me, or maybe you need to look for other qualities than those you've been stuck on.

You try to say, okay, well, I know that this person did something wrong, but maybe it wasn't that they were doing something wrong. Maybe I did something to cause that. Maybe I need someone else, just not that person.

In those situations, it's common to recycle the pattern through different people, through different situations. May not have that same issue the same way, but you recycle the pattern because you're not dealing with why it's frustrating. You're not dealing with why you keep getting into that situation.

If the mindset has not been dealt with, how you're getting the result means that you will continue to do the same thing, thinking that you will get a different result because you're intellectualizing what has gone wrong to make that situation not work. So instead of addressing the situation or the reason behind it and how to tweak what you're doing to get a better result, you make an educated excuse for why the result didn't come out as it should. And it'll be blaming everything, but you need to re-strategize what you're doing.

Sublimation

The last and healthiest of these defense mechanisms is sublimation. Sublimation involves turning a negative into a positive. Instead of feeling anger and allowing that anger to provoke you into violence or negative speech, you harness that energy and transform it into something positive.

This could manifest as a song, poetry, or another creative outlet to channel that energy. Diverting energy in this way is completely valid, as it can help address some of the issues we're discussing. When I say resolve, I mean we can apply sublimation to navigate these defense mechanisms.

This process involves learning to reframe a situation into a more positive one by crafting a positive narrative and altering the story you've been told or have internalized. The narrative you receive is yours to reshape. So, if someone irritates you or someone steps on your toes, or if someone makes an unkind remark.

Instead of getting frustrated with that person, you can take that frustration and turn it into something positive, allowing you to build a new foundation based on what you dislike. You can start to fight against the causes of your frustrations. You begin to advocate for a positive insight or outlook on something that bothers you. Turning a negative into a positive is sublimation.

We want to focus on this as we begin to work through these band-aids, also known as defense mechanisms. These particular defense mechanisms serve as mental band-aids that we navigate when we exhibit behaviors associated with them. So, there are the defense mechanisms that pertain to the mental aspect of these coping strategies. Then, there are the external band-aids used to cover up issues that need to be addressed and processed. However, we will address those matters right after this.

Section 4: Understanding and Walking Your Path

The Judas Theory, a lesson in grace, comes in two parts following this introduction to the section.

The two parts include Part 1, recognizing who you are and knowing your assignment, capabilities, and genuine heart intent. Your life was preplanned with a purpose. Part 2 is knowing that everything in your life is aligned with God's plans.

There are no mistakes, only lessons, as each of us learns at our own pace along various paths filled with grace for our life's purpose. Since there are no mistakes, we can all adapt and seek forgiveness. Making necessary changes allows us to avoid self-condemnation for the struggles faced in overcoming our challenges. In both sections, we will explore our life experiences and how they have shaped our identities.

Understanding our life experiences and their role in our journey towards righteousness reveals how grace can cultivate us. If we process these experiences effectively, we can learn from each one. This, in turn, transforms us at the soul level, aligning our behavior patterns with the grace present in our lives.

First, let's define *grace*.

By definition, grace is a simple elegance or refinement of movement, courteous goodwill, and due honor or credit granted to something or someone by one's presence. Now, my understanding of grace, in this book on spiritual human behavior, describes grace as the inherent plan or path we all possess. We are born into a particular environment that shapes the plan, path, and purpose we are meant to experience in this life. Grace represents the amount of wiggle room you are allowed based on your circumstances, life experiences, and the environment into which you were placed, enabling you to succeed regardless of the challenges.

Based on your gift, calling, life assignment, and purpose, whatever your purpose may be, there is a grace that allows you to experience situations that provide lessons and lead to inevitable "mistakes" that may appear as mistakes on the surface but serve a deeper purpose on a spiritual level. Grace gives you the leeway and space to adjust, the room to grow, and the opportunity to make "mistakes," enabling you to recognize where you need to develop.

This chapter is titled the Judas theory because it explores Judas's mindset and misunderstanding of grace. In the biblical narrative, Judas is one of Jesus' 12 disciples, who faced the dilemma of betraying his leader for money. He was asked if he would expose Jesus' location in exchange for this payment.

He prioritized monetary gain over his Savior and spiritual leader in making this deal. By making such an exchange, he believed he had stepped outside of God's will and committed an irredeemable sin. However, if he had grasped the concept of grace, he could have returned to Jesus for forgiveness and possibly saved Jesus from being murdered.

However, the accurate picture of Judas to himself is misunderstood because he didn't stay long enough to vindicate himself. He failed to change his behavior so that Jesus would no longer be compromised. I mean, he tried to return. But by the time he did, it was already too late. They didn't want him back. They didn't want the money; they wanted the person.

It's essential to understand Judas based on the concept that all the disciples sometimes disregarded Jesus. At some point, all the disciples turned their backs on Jesus. However, Judas was the only disciple who decided that he could not live with the type of betrayal that he committed against Jesus.

Many might ask, how did they all walk away? When Jesus was taken away, none of his disciples said, "I'm his disciple, don't harm him." Instead, they all denied him, chose their paths, and scattered. Were they dispersing to protect the gospel? Or were they only concerned with their safety? Or were they no better than Judas, opting not to end their own lives but seeking redemption later?

This whole theory is about shifting the mindset and the condemnation that says you must be like Judas if you make a mistake, as most people view mistakes as the betrayal of Judas. Some will treat you like you've committed the ultimate sin if you make a mistake. If by chance you do something that does not align with what people believe you should do, then they think you are out of the will of God. However, the thought process behind creating this chapter is that Judas was in the will of God the entire time; Judas was meant to betray Jesus, and Jesus knew Judas was going to betray him. Still, Judas struggled with his assignment, according to what Jesus already knew was going to happen.

If you have a particular assignment, you must understand, accept, embrace, and be willing to pursue your assignment without self-sabotaging your entire life. This self-sabotage can prevent you from seeing the rewards of your harvest and hinder your ability to manifest what you desire in a way that transforms your behavior. Judas was remorseful; he regretted his actions. However, the guilt of not understanding his purpose, his walk, and his assignment led him to take his own life, based on the story of the bible.

Chapter 7: The Judas Theory (A Lesson in Grace)

Part one

The previous chapters, How the Mind Works, God's Will, Parental Influences, God's Provisional System, Free Will, the Hold-Up Theory, and the Band-Aid Effect, are essential to establish part one. If you've gone through all those chapters, for those of you who are doing the lesson plan and completing the journal workbooks, they would have caused you to evaluate yourself on a deeper level and from a deeper perspective, so that you can understand your journey.

This is important because, depending on how your mindset has been shaped, the will of God and purpose for your individual life, along with your gifts, skills, talents, and the purposeful plan you are designed to fulfill in this lifetime, as well as how your parents and your parental or guardian influences have shaped your mind, contribute to the things you'd like to change in each of these areas.

Additionally, understanding your free will is crucial to grasping the concept of reclaiming your understanding and walking out your path, reclaiming your life, understanding your purpose, and pursuing the journey toward your greatness and divine plan. Delving into the Hold-Up Theory and Baid-Aids unlocks the key to changing your behavior patterns.

Changing your behavioral pattern begins with determining your goals, understanding your purpose, and recognizing your divine plan based on your prayers to God. Additionally, identify what prevents you from fulfilling that divine plan and what stops or distracts you from being focused, committed, and manifesting what you truly believe in.

The Hold-Up and Band-Aid Theories are examples of the many distractions that can disrupt God's perfect plan for your life, which are often noticed once you reflect on them. A perfect plan for your life does not necessarily mean that it won't be filled with challenges that people mistake for errors, depending on what your life is destined to be, what you're meant to become, what you are called to do, and your purpose in this world.

Once you recognize the band-aid effect and acknowledge the' positive and negative aspects of actions, it's essential to see how these can mask our need for healing. For instance, what might seem like a benefit of attending church excessively, like feeling connected, can be a temporary fix. If you merely indulge in church without confronting your inner struggles, it becomes a superficial solution, creating an illusion that everything is fine. Meanwhile, you overlook the need to address your problems and seek genuine healing by reflecting on yourself.

All those things lead us to section four, chapter seven, part one, where you recognize yourself through all those other experiences while knowing that you have a specific assignment. You were placed on earth at this time to achieve something great. Your greatness may be simply healing or breaking a generational curse, mending the wounds of your parents through your life and the lives of your children. When you have a child as a mother or a father, that child provides love, direction, and a sense of purpose, adding meaning and creating value in your life (if you allow it).

Once you realize this, you can pursue life a little better and differently. Many people need love, support, admiration, and various things from their children when they become parents. Often, they neglect their children in search of Love, support, and other experiences that their children provide.

Imagine if you evolve to implement essential changes that offer your children a different experience. In doing so, you have shattered a generational curse that has plagued your family. By dismantling these issues, you can create a fresh beginning. The aim is to acknowledge your mission.

Whether your assignment is something vast that will reach around the world or something limited to your family, it depends on how you heal, process, and overcome any experience you've faced. Each experience will lead you to where you're meant to be.

Many events happen in cycles. In these cycles, you might observe that a parent experiences something, and the child encounters the same situation. For instance, my ex-husband once stepped on an object that completely pierced his foot as a child. A few years ago, our son experienced a similar near-miss when his foot was slightly pierced by an object outside. Thankfully, he was not hurt to the same extent as his dad's experience.

The moment it occurred, it reminded me of the cycle and what his dad experienced. It felt like a revelation. It was a valuable learning experience for me because I believe in cycles. One is likely to face the same challenges their parents encountered.

How you respond to it determines the impact your decisions will have on your life compared to your past decisions. Later, in the paradox chapter, we will explore the process of breaking cycles. In discussing paradoxes, we will examine cycles, break cycles, and make new choices to overcome generational curses.

Let's get back to the Judas theory. My theory and belief as a soul is that we all come to earth, born with a purpose, whether in animal form, plant form, human form, or any other form that can be presented as a living organism here on earth. Now, because we are all souls, we all come to earth with a purpose and a plan.

In a previous chapter, we discussed the theory that we have pre-planned a journey here on Earth. Some of this belief comes from the Bible, while others arise simply from observing the course of life. We recognize that if we are born into a particular environment or situation, unless we emerge from a context that ceased to exist, we are all here to evolve, not only ourselves but also the Earth and the environment around us. This evolution occurs through the understanding that before you came to Earth, you were provided with a mother and a father, alongside a review of life's potential paths.

There are two options within this journey of life. You're either going to move on instinct, or you're going to move very randomly and sporadically. Moving on instinct is akin to acting based on your intuition, understanding the world around you, and how the universe speaks to you directly.

Moving spontaneously means acting on the emotional cues from others that trigger you to move, prompted solely by somebody else's actions, inaction, words, or silence. We believe that you and your life were predestined before your arrival on earth, shaped by your parents and the circumstances of your birth.

We developed the Judas theory to understand grace, recognizing that the course of life assigned to you influences how you process, comprehend, and apply lessons from every experience encountered, endured, and learned from during this time.
First, you must take responsibility for who you are, your thoughts, and your daily actions. Regardless of your origin, background, or past, if you're over 18, you hold complete control over your life and its direction. Acknowledge that if you disliked that experience, you must forge a new one by altering your actions to influence your behavior.

Not every experience or outcome arises from our mistakes. Yet, regardless of whether we've erred, it's crucial to acknowledge our role in shaping our identity. If you start to recognize traits you're unhappy with—such as drinking, smoking, or drug use—or realize something unsatisfactory about yourself, like a negative attitude, dependency on others, or the need to prove your worth, taking charge of your life and identity transforms everything.

By embracing responsibility for who you are, you recognize that although your upbringing may have influenced you, you are not destined to be merely a product of that upbringing. The undesirable traits are adaptations for survival in response to the people and situations you have encountered.

What can I do now to change that? How do I change how I deal with where I come from? Do I hang on to the adverse effects of my background? Or do I take this time to evaluate and reflect on how this can change and evolve me for the better, without being led astray by anything resembling selling out the gospel or compromising my leader or my spiritual oneness with God?

If you sell out your spiritual connection with God. It can corrupt your heart because you are then led by what that selling-out feeling does to you, rather than your intuitive instincts that guide you according to what God has in store for you, not based on the financial narrative. Therefore, you must take responsibility for who you are, where you are, why you are, and how you behave daily. The goal and purpose of spiritual human behavior is to help you shape your life according to your desired outcomes and beliefs.

You pattern your life based on your thoughts, and that pattern shapes your behavior. Changing the way you view life, how you look at life, how you look at how you were raised, and looking for the lessons within every situation that seemed like a trial, finding the lesson in every situation that seemed like it was sent to break you. Because if you find the lesson, you will see where it was sent to make you. If you avoid the lesson and the responsibility, you will continue to face similar things that make you face yourself and take responsibility for yourself, who you are, and how you think.

Now, you must understand that the things you went through in your childhood are not necessarily your fault. But how you react to those things and allow those you overcame to survive throughout your childhood and adolescence are the things you can look at and say, "You know what? I didn't like this experience." I didn't like this narrative.

What will I do to change how that has shaped me? Those same struggles and trials can be a blessing if you seek the lessons in them, despite what you've gone through. Every lesson you find within this chapter may not necessarily apply directly to your life, especially when addressing childhood traumas and discovering lessons, particularly if you have a history of abusing your childhood and adolescence.

If you have a history of neglect, which is a form of abuse, or any form of spiritual neglect, this too is a type of abuse. If you've faced struggles, trials, or complicated situations during your upbringing, any hardships you experienced were meant to bless, help, and shape you. However, you must take responsibility for addressing those issues.

If you were molested, you may not be able to articulate what lesson you've learned from yourself in that situation, as someone took your innocence. Nonetheless, you can learn how to protect the innocence of others; you can use that to help you understand your movements and operations based on that.

Every experience shapes you and your outlook; every negative experience leaves an imprint on your mind and heart. Whether you avoid that imprint or process it and grow from it is a responsibility you must accept when you become accountable for your life and purpose. However, amidst these challenges, you also have to recognize the flaws within yourself and correct them.

Being uptight is not necessarily a flaw if you experience something that makes you more uptight. You must review what made you skeptical if you are mean, aggressive, undermining, and skeptical of everything. Every action reacts.

When was the first time you had that reaction? When did you first become skeptical? When was the first time you realized a flaw wasn't always a physical mark or a blemish? It may just be your defense mechanism kicking in. Your flaw could be that you don't let people get close enough to honestly know them, to give them a chance to be close to you, or to become friends.

It's a flaw, not due to the circumstances that made you this way, but because of the inability to grow in that area. It's like a mistake. Mistakes aren't mistakes. If you learn a lesson from what you did and didn't like, it's only a mistake when you dislike the result. If you like the result, it is not a mistake.

If you continue doing it the same way and receive the same results, that's a decision, not a mistake. There's nothing wrong with making decisions as long as you're growing with, from, and for the choices you start to make.

Don't do anything now that could lead to an outcome you won't like five years from now. If five years from now means you will be a certain way or have a specific impact on your life, you need to change your thinking and challenge your mindset based on those factors and times. Next, avoid associating with those who misalign your actions and thoughts.

Remember, we talked about the integrity factor. Within the integrity factor, it's simply about being a good person because you are a good person. It's about being honest, even when nobody is looking. Integrity means doing what's right because it's right, even if nobody else thinks it's right; you know it's right because it is. Understanding integrity and living by the integrity factor will help you manage your life, allowing you to avoid worrying about whether you've hurt someone.

It's treating people the way that you would like to be treated. If you treat yourself at the absolute highest standard of being treated. What you accept and how you see yourself and treat yourself is based on the people you place around you.

If you look around, the five people you spend the most time with will affect where you see yourself going. So, who do you spend most of your time with? Are they suitable for your mental, spiritual, and financial health? Are they suitable for your physical health? Are they beneficial for your evolution and growth? Do they influence you positively? Do they uplift you? Do they encourage you? Do they help you think better? Do they help you think more broadly? Do they assist you in reaching new levels of achievement? Those factors are essential. You should not associate with people whose actions or thoughts contradict God's will for your life, goals, and plans.

Many people have decided to pressure others into purchasing classes or taking courses they believe will help them succeed. However, being coerced into buying and attending these classes may not align with God's unique plan for your life. Trying to conform to someone else's path, even if it appears beneficial and aligned, could lead to misalignment. If it is not divinely designed as your course of action or means of escape, what may have worked for others could hinder your growth. It can obstruct what God is trying to accomplish or redirect you down a path that ultimately delays His intentions.

You must ensure the people around you can help you manifest supportive individuals who can pray for and with you—people who won't discuss your problems in a way that does not help anyone evolve from the conversation. It is also essential to evaluate what is purposeful for you, so that you can recognize when others are trying to manipulate your innocence or take advantage of you. When I mentioned people buying classes, many seek money; they've been broke all their lives, and their only goal is not to be broke.

There is nothing wrong with wanting financial freedom or success. However, what another person seeks in life may not be meaningful to you. Therefore, the goal you need to focus on is creating your objectives and determining which actions will align with what you believe is your purpose in this life and what's on your goal list.

If you aim to be a showgirl in Vegas, moving to Dubai and never auditioning in Vegas may not be purposeful, especially if it doesn't align with your goals. Remember, you could meet someone in Dubai recruiting for showgirls in Vegas.

Given Dubai's heritage, history, and atmosphere, the chances of securing a show booking in Vegas as a showgirl are pretty slim. However, this doesn't mean you shouldn't travel to Dubai, nor does it imply that traveling there means you can't pursue a career as a showgirl.

If being a showgirl is your goal, you should take the steps necessary to align yourself with that aspiration. If by chance you aim to become a renowned, best-selling author who wins Nobel Peace Prizes, it is essential to be in environments that cater to your desires. To become an author, you must immerse yourself in settings encouraging you to think about the topics you wish to write about.

You need to research and develop the theories leading to winning the Nobel Peace Prize. You should be actively working toward becoming an author and achieving that accolade, which does not include, or perhaps it does for you, pursuing a career as a stripper. A showgirl and a stripper are two distinct roles, and I respect those involved in the adult entertainment business.

However, unless you have a way of stripping that will bring peace to the entire world, being a stripper is not as purposeful on your path to winning a Noble Prize as studying in school or pursuing private study of all the information that interests you, which could help you win or be awarded the Nobel Prize. What is purposeful for you? What are your goals? What do you wish to accomplish? How do you reach those goals and accomplishments? What path should you take? What course of action is needed now to discover what is purposeful? Stripping and the Nobel Prize are just a few examples.

To find what is purposeful, you may need some time for meditation and silence, where you are removed from distractions, people, or anything that could prevent you from formulating your plan. When you evaluate and remain purposeful, you are crafting your plan, weighing your costs, and determining what it will take to achieve the goals you have set for yourself. What will it take to fulfill the purpose you believe you were born on Earth to complete? Then, you must recognize when others are attempting to manipulate your innocence.

The world is filled with various types of people: good, not-so-good, and horrible. Even good individuals may seek to use you for your resources, which doesn't inherently make them bad. However, manipulation occurs when someone is not being straightforward. Instead of being honest, they may employ indirect tactics solely for their gain. This behavior often arises from a desire to exploit your innocence or something you view as innocent.

That means you may not have a bad bone in your body. Because you don't have any bad intentions regarding your finances and are willing to spend quickly, some people may exploit your financial vulnerability to take advantage of you. Since you'll spend your money anyway, they want you to spend it all on them, and it's not bad.

But if that person were not trying to manipulate your innocence, they would give you tips on saving money, not just buying everything you're offered. It's about having discernment and a sense of self-control. Much of what we see here in this Judas part one involves self-control, learning how to manage yourself, and gaining insight into yourself to allow you to take control of your life, including the alignment of your life and the people you permit.

You need to identify your motives and those of those around you and examine whether money can influence your judgment. I discussed this briefly regarding the courses I mentioned, where people often target those who are more naive or less knowledgeable. I've even heard someone say, "We're charging people for being lazy."

When ill-informed, people often lack the knowledge necessary to seek answers independently. Rather than guiding you to the information you need for free, they charge a fee, making you pay for not understanding how to find those answers. Not everyone is lazy.

Some individuals don't know where to begin. When you lack direction, you seek help. If you're desperate enough while looking for assistance, you're willing to do anything to embark on the path you're eager to start.

It is essential that you check your motivation. If you're looking for money, people will rob you of all your wealth. Those who spend all their money to get rich quickly are the same individuals who end up broke ten years later. People who win the lottery often end up broke because their motivation and intention were never to do anything fruitful with it; they simply aimed to accumulate wealth for spending.

Typically, if you allow money to dictate your actions and behaviors, you can be bought if the price is right. If the price is right, someone can persuade you to do something you wouldn't typically do without money's influence. The objective is not to be driven solely by money, with it always tied to your decisions.

Learn to be subjective, be objective, and say no, even when there's money involved, even if it's amounts that you've never been exposed to before that you can never have without doing that. If it's meant for you, God will bring it to you. God is not telling you to sell your purpose to make a few bucks.

God does not want you to accept any hogwash that someone tries to sell you about their methods, suggesting that if you don't follow them, it won't work. Even as you read this book and digest this information, spiritual human behavior aims to identify who you are as an individual. It involves becoming the best version of yourself based on what you like and want to do, what feels right, what makes you happy, and what is meaningful to you through your soul connection with God.

You must come to terms with yourself, understand precisely who you are and why you are that way, and use this understanding to take accountability and responsibility for yourself.

How does this portion relate to Judas? Judas took money to betray his leader. If you take money to sell your leader out for financial gains, then that is what leads you to be controlled by money. Judas' situation and background may have influenced his decision to do so.

You never know what goes on in people's minds that motivates them to be driven by money, beyond just being cash poor. Additionally, you must be willing to apologize when you've done or said something wrong, without regrets. And here's the thing: there's nothing wrong with getting help or seeking advice and paying for someone to assist you.

There is nothing wrong with making a wise investment in yourself and in information that will help you grow mentally and spiritually, without being sold the ideal of God or the notion of something else, but simply by learning and understanding yourself. Suppose you find yourself in a situation where you are compromising on the things you hold dear, which are true for your spiritual journey on earth. In that case, you need to be willing to apologize, but this doesn't necessarily mean apologizing to others. However, apologizing is very important if you have wronged someone because it allows you and others to move towards forgiveness.

You also have to apologize to yourself when you make a decision that leads to a result you're not pleased with. You need to be willing to say, "You know what? That's not going to get me to where I want to go. Let's rethink how we're going to do this."

You must be open to changing your behavior patterns, especially when they consistently yield results that leave you unhappy. So, if, before you bought a course, you didn't learn anything and all they did was share their stories, they didn't provide any foundational tips to help you grow your soul. Next time, you need to focus on growing your soul without regrets. Don't regret where you've made an error or a decision that led to something unfavorable. Instead, concentrate on realignment, being readjusted, and clearing out the old to build the new. Remove anything that doesn't contribute to your growth.

If Judas could have improved his actions from part one, he should have questioned why he was associating with people who disliked his friend. If they are not aligned with your purpose, it's best to distance yourself. When you feel unmotivated to fulfill your responsibilities, it's essential to align with people who will push you forward, encourage you, and be a beacon of hope, instead of individuals who don't mean well. This will allow you to embrace your true self.

Part 2

Recognizing that all aspects of your life fit within God's predetermined plan is essential. Factors such as your birthplace, family background, and environment influence your circumstances, leading you to specific points in your journey. Opportunities and situations arise at specific times or places, which might appear incorrect, misaligned, or misguided to you.

Trust that you're not ignoring your intuition, which tells you not to do certain things. You must accept whatever God allows you to encounter, whatever God permits you to see, and whatever God enables you to become. At each junction in the road that God leads you to, you should be willing to choose a path, not necessarily the safest or the most dangerous.

Still, you must be willing to pray and choose a path to fulfill what you are called, destined, and purposed to do on this earth. It's essential to realize that everything in your life aligns with God's plan. Evaluate the current aspects of your life to see if they make you happy, nurture your growth, and help you move closer to your goals.

If those things feed your growth and help you get closer to your current goals, how will they play out now, and how will they play out 2345 years from now? The goal is to have a clear list of objectives, dreams, or wishes—things you plan to do or pray to God to come true. If you approach this through prayer, meditation, and self-examination, you will gain a plan and a list of goals you wish to accomplish.

Conversely, you will also see who you are and what you need to do to change what may be blocking your way. I have to foolproof this because I don't want you to go against what you know is wrong to say you're trying to reach a goal. Please don't force it. Don't force anything in your life from this point forward. I'm not saying things should always be laid out and handed to you.

What I will tell you is that there is a law of attraction, a law of provision, a law of love that rules the land. If you are willing to get to know, accept, and embrace yourself, you will begin to attract what you need. Things will become easier as you attract what you need into your life.

As situations become easier, you will no longer need to force yourself into circumstances that could be detrimental later. When attempting to handle things by forcing outcomes, figuring things out, and making everything work, you ultimately find yourself in situations or binds that don't truly serve you. The best way to avoid this is by knowing your plan, understanding what will benefit it, and identifying what actions you need to take to reach the promised land and get to the other side.

You're probably asking, how does this relate to the Judas story in theory?

The connection to the Judas story can be found by examining the Last Supper, when Jesus and the 12 disciples gathered, during which Judas learned of the impending betrayal. This revelation may have planted a seed in his mind, ultimately enabling him to feel at ease before regretting his actions. Jesus had foretold this would happen, giving Judas a moment to reconsider.

That was the opportunity for Judas to recall Jesus saying it would come to pass, and he would have to face this issue. Judas could have done what might be considered the proper thing. When that opportunity arises, choose differently, change the path of the future, and alter the past cycle by changing the outcome.

In part one, we discussed how to break cycles of generational curses and the necessary actions to stop a cycle you may find yourself in—whether in relationships, family matters, personal life, or business. Every day, you encounter specific cycles and patterns. You can either repeat the same choices you usually make or choose a different path.

The aspiration is to make a different choice to achieve a different outcome. When Jesus mentioned someone would betray him, he had already indicated he would be killed days earlier. Paul insisted that this would not occur.

Jesus replied, "Hold on, Paul. I am aware this is destined to happen. Because I know what's meant to unfold, I want to give you a warning as it likely will take place." This was the day when he first received the vision, heard it from God, and chose to share it with someone.

From that moment, they had multiple chances to divert, intervene, or stop the process. Their first chance arose during that conversation, during which he informed Paul of what was to come, yet they did not alter their path.

At the dinner table, Jesus expressed, "Hey, this is what I feel will happen. This is what my intuition, the Creator, the universe, and the Father God are telling me in my soul will occur in this environment with the people surrounding me." It was a pivotal moment for intervention.

Even Judas had his moment to intervene when he heard those things. Then he had another chance to act. Judas had the opportunity to intervene again when he went there. During this time, he had the chance to act, and when presented with the money, he could have reconsidered, recalling the warning.

After he took the money, he could still have gone back to warn Jesus's disciples to save, hide, and protect him. Judas had three chances to fix the issue, try to correct it, prevent it, or intervene.

The last opportunity for Jesus to intervene came when Peter could have fought with those men. However, before it escalated, Jesus chose to pray. Rather than praying and escaping the hands of his captors, he remained there. He prayed and chastised the other disciples for dozing off instead of staying vigilant. Jesus consistently evaded capture. He skillfully dodged various situations until he faced a moment when a friend betrayed him in a seemingly unforgivable manner.

Reflecting on this, I consider a perspective that offers Judas grace. If Judas had returned to seek God's forgiveness and guidance on how to mend what he believed he had destroyed, he might have found redemption, despite everything already being part of God's plan. Jesus was aware of what would transpire and was mentally prepared for it, as he had foreseen these events.

I won't address his anticipation of his death and resurrection. He knew he was destined for the cross and the accompanying challenges. He also foresaw Peter's denial. When he realized Peter would deny him, he said, "I know you're going to deny me. It's alright. I'll let you know exactly when it will happen."

He explained, "When you hear the crows, you will deny me. This indicates you have denied me three times." When this occurred in the Bible, Peter realized he had made a mistake, as Jesus had foretold. Despite his actions, he was forgiven and achieved more, as it was part of God's plan.

He needed to reach a point of no return—or, should I say, life after death—because there is indeed a point of return mentioned in the Bible's stories. Jesus understood that all these events had to unfold based on the Bible's words for us to be free. Jesus would have been aware that Judas would either take his own life or disappear, unable to face the shame of his wrongdoing, which was part of the mission to liberate people. Well, at least based on Christian belief, Jesus was born so that he would die to save the world.

When contemplating the chapter "Judas: A Lesson in Grace," it's crucial to understand that it doesn't imply you should betray someone and seek forgiveness afterward. Instead, this chapter emphasizes that there are no mistakes in your journey toward your destination. The path designed by God for you to experience on earth contains no mistakes, only lessons that guide you in awakening to your true self at the soul level. Recognizing this is vital. This perspective allows us to avoid shame, guilt, and anxiety when reflecting on our actions.

The Bible teaches that God knows all the joys and hardships in our lives from start to finish. He knew us even before we were conceived, suggesting that our souls met with God before our earthly life, who imparted a purpose—a mission tailored for each of us. This purpose includes being placed in our specific families, with full knowledge of the experiences, challenges, and encounters we would face and everything we would say, do, and become. Our destined journey is clearly defined before birth, but we must remember through prayer, meditation, Deja vu, and dreams.

Imagine taking a crash course that allows you to review your assignment before a big test.

At the start of the course, the instructions start with:

"When you arrive on Earth, you must remember that this is the plan for your life. Some aspects of this plan are designed to awaken your soul, helping you recall. Try not to sleep too long or too deeply when you get to Earth. Avoid being confused by what is happening in that world. I need you to remember this plan of action so that when you come into your mother's womb, you can learn to walk and talk. That's a part of the Earth plan. Then, guess what? As you begin to experience these things listed here and meet these people, this is the area you will be in.

These are the things you are going to enjoy doing. You will encounter this experience, whether good, bad, or indifferent. All the possibilities are right here. Can you commit to this? When you descend into your mother's womb and emerge on the other side, your task is to remember who you are. Know that I am the author and the finisher of your faith and that everything you need, you can receive from me.

All you have to do is ask. All you have to do is seek salvation within yourself. Because this plan I'm presenting to you now, before you enter your mother's womb, is matchless. Everything is already worked out. No matter what you do or say, the result will still be the result.

But let me warn you, some challenges will be scary when you get down to earth. It's going to be kind of like, you know, where you can get close to death and not die. However, your contract will end eventually, and you will return here.

When on Earth, your soul contracts, and your life plan will be slightly adjusted. You'll experience some of the same things, endure challenges, overcome obstacles, and face the fears you have. From there, you will discover everything in this paperwork.

Could you agree to it? If everything goes well, your carrier takes care of their body, and everybody plays their part, then this should go well. So now that they're getting ready, we have hooked them up and created that schedule for them to connect, meet, and do this. All of this was in your parents' soul plans. But now, here is your plan. When you arrive on Earth, please stick to this plan.

It's not going to be easy. You may enter the world born into everything that's in this plan. All you have to do is awaken it within yourself. Come to yourself, know yourself, understand yourself, learn more about who you are, what you like, and why you like it, then accept and adjust. Know that when you pray and meditate, you can connect to your purpose and the Source of all to continue on your journey.

When the time comes, you will return to me when you become a pure soul again and are released from the Earth's atmosphere. If your mission was incomplete, you will return to Earth soon."

This highlights the significance of the soul agreement: recognizing your preordained life plan. You have already determined your purpose, identity, and how to utilize your experiences. Initiating the healing that will facilitate your soul's next growth phase is essential, which is what spiritual human behavior is all about.

There are no mistakes, only lessons, as we all learn at our own pace. Nobody has this thing called life perfect, as everybody has different perspectives, understandings, experiences, parents, and upbringings. For example, two children can live in the same house and sometimes experience life differently.

Don't get caught up in what everyone else is doing around you. Understanding who you are will help you connect with God directly and ignite the source within you. Gathering with other believers who view life similarly is excellent if you need fellowship. Both will contribute to helping you grow, pursue your purpose, mature, and develop your spiritual behavior. Since there are no mistakes, we can all be forgiven when we make the necessary life adjustments.

Making the proper life adjustments isn't a science, so we shouldn't condemn ourselves for the things we struggle to fix within ourselves. The most important thing to understand about spiritual human behavior is that everything involves healing, hearing, and feeling God's guidance on your life. If you recognize that your life was already planned and that there are no mistakes—only lessons to learn and actions you must take to learn those lessons, it will shift how you see things.

If you fail to learn the lesson, it will return in different ways and forms. The key aspect of the Judas theory is recognizing that if something is included in your divine plan, grace is available to help you through it. Therefore, I urge you not to weigh yourself down with stress, as it can lead to illness. Excessive stress can lead to further health problems. Avoid putting pressure on yourself due to mistakes; both literally and figuratively, do not cause yourself harm.

If you are considering suicide, it does not end the problems in your life; instead, it creates new issues and inflicts hurt and pain on the lives of those who love and care for you. They may struggle to express it, but their feelings for you are deep and impactful, ultimately bringing you joy and a sense of worth. Before you commit to harming yourself physically or stressing yourself mentally, spiritually, or financially, I want you to know that there is nothing you have done that God cannot forgive. You are a product of your environment.

If you are struggling with thoughts of self-harm, please call 988 for help!

No matter what you face, it's time for you to take responsibility and accountability for who you are, where you are, and, more importantly, where you want to be. Now, I'm not trying to fuss. This is for your growth.

If you're reading this, I want you to look up reflexology, numerology, and chakras and understand the effects of unbalanced chakras on your body. Certain factors, if you're not balanced within yourself, your heart, your mind, and your intuition, can make you sick, and we don't want that.

That's why we don't want you to stress; our motto is no stress. Identify what causes you stress and reduce it. If it's people or things you can distance yourself from or eliminate, so be it.

The goal is to lead a life where you don't constantly explain yourself and don't feel judged for the choices you've made or for managing the life you've had thus far. Recognize that every challenge you encounter is part of a larger plan for your growth.

As you seek out the lessons and blessings in your experiences, you will attract even more blessings, as the lessons are truly the blessings. These lessons represent some of your greatest gifts, transforming your behavior and facilitating your healing.

This allows you to see yourself within yourself and make the necessary adjustments so that you don't have to worry about your past actions or the potential bad karma that may arise. When you recognize a particular pattern, you can correct it to prevent yourself from falling into negative cycles. By identifying these patterns, you can adjust your behavior to avoid repeating the same path and experiencing the same unwanted results.

You should also remember that nobody is truly perfect. According to human standards, there are literally no perfect people on this earth.

Even when you think of Jesus, he ran away from home, spoke back to his parents, and broke every law that the Pharisees and the leaders of his time told him not to break. He challenged everything they said and did everything they instructed him not to do. He was God's son, and God was well pleased with him.

Adversity does not mean you are outside God's plan if you encounter it. It could be a lesson you must endure to learn and grow into the person you are meant to be. Understand that the person who judges you may not have overcome their struggles or be aware of their denials. Anyone who has truly faced adversity and emerged from it begins to see life in a different light.

Unless they condemn themselves for their past, they'll see you and think they can't judge you because they've experienced similar situations. This understanding allows them to let you live and learn from your experiences.

Anyone who truly loves you will not make you feel guilty about your past actions. They might hold you accountable, which can feel unpleasant at times. They can also recognize your responsibility for specific outcomes. However, being held accountable for your involvement can be uncomfortable, especially if you're unhappy with the results.

However, it's essential to recognize that no one is without flaws. Jesus made mistakes, Peter had his faults, and Paul faced difficulties, including being shipwrecked. Peter cut off a man's ear. Consider David; he was indeed flawed, murdering for his marital desires. He took multiple wives, just like many others of his time. Yet he was considered a man after God's heart. Abraham also faced moral challenges—everyone had their struggles.

Moses had his issues. He didn't speak well. He did not want to do the work because he didn't know how to accomplish it due to his speech difficulties, but God had someone else already prepared to do the talking for him. Every person who has achieved something great has made what others might view as mistakes. At the same time, it was perfect for God's plan and perfect will for their lives.

Every message in the Bible originated as a misinterpretation or perceived mistake, yet God had a purpose for each one. No matter your challenges, understand that there is a purpose behind them if you can learn from these situations, whether to protect your children or break a generational cycle of behavior. Making the necessary changes and adjustments to your mindset regarding your actions might cause you to regret certain things, but don't let it lead to self-doubt.

Acknowledge your negative feelings about the outcome, and learn how to avoid repeating the same mistakes that cause you distress.

God has the power to restore you once you engage with Him mentally. By engaging mentally, I refer to the idea of having a soul contract and mission before your arrival on Earth—the divine plan for your life conceived before you entered your mother's womb. If you pause to seek this understanding, God will remind you of that purpose and reveal it.

However, you need to be open to listening, learning, and accepting what God reveals to you, even when it's uncomfortable or not widely accepted. If others criticize or stare at you oddly, remember that if you assist someone in overcoming a serious challenge, facilitating their healing, or uplifting their spirit, you will face judgment simply because you are different.

Understand that God can use you because He knows that if He helps you, you will give all the glory to Him. You're going to tell everybody how you connected with your inner soul, and that it was a God experience within. This links you with God on a Jesus level by renewing your mindset about how God would have you move and operate, and the things that Jesus was trying to spread, helping others understand who God is. Coming into alignment with yourself and taking some time for yourself is essential. When Judas ran off and killed himself, he should have instead spent some time praying.

He was a disciple who had learned to pray, believe, and have faith. However, when the pressure mounted, he didn't know how to save himself or seek God's guidance to become his best self and atone for his past actions.

Like Paul and Peter, he could have supported Jesus' mission. Yet, if God's plan was for Jesus to die at that moment, Judas fulfilled his role, regardless of how it felt; that was his contribution to the mission. He may have found clarity if he prayed for forgiveness and recognized that Jesus had foreseen their journey.

If he foretold that we would go through it, it had to be meant for me to do it. Because in order to get to the other side, this had to be done. Instead of condemning yourself or thinking that you did something wrong, ask God why He allowed it. How does that shape your plan for life? And how does that shape your life plan, the things you were called to do, and the things you would do in your future long term?

You must believe that God preplanned you before you arrived on Earth. One of your main goals now is to remember God's plan for you. Right now, ask God what the plan is for your life. Before I entered my mother's womb? When you sent me to Earth, what did you envision for me? What would you have me do? Let that inspire your vision board and goals, and allow the meditation from that prayer to guide you to where you're meant to go.

If you pray and then the next day, you are on a different vibe that aligns with what you pray for, then take that as a sign from God to continue in that direction. One of the most important parts is getting all the discontent and hate out of your heart and filling it with gratitude, peace, and forgiveness.

This may mean getting rid of some people or stopping going to specific places to maintain peace. It means escaping drama, catty behavior, and gossiping about things that will not help better the earth, the planet, or anything else. But don't tear other people down.

Free your mind, free your heart, and live on to be great. You don't have to die emotionally, physically, sexually, spiritually, financially, or in any way. Once you begin to know yourself and explore yourself, you unlock deeper levels of your soul. Accepting everything about you helps you become a better version of yourself. No one is better than you. We are all different. We all have flaws.

Believe in yourself. Even if nobody else believes in you, you must begin to accept and believe in yourself. Now I do want to note this source.

Understanding suicidal behavior and symptoms affecting the mind, body, heart, and soul involves ensuring you maintain positive energy, surround yourself with the right people, and focus your mind on meaningful pursuits. Rather than watching reality TV, scripted shows, or unscripted programs, it takes time to explore the questions that occupy your mind. Consider it seriously if you have a question, no matter how foolish you might think it is.

It is essential to be able to research anything. The website and mobile app offer information about religion, spirituality, personal growth, and psychology, and there are plenty of resources to help you.

Take some time to research the important things to you. What's the randomest thing that crossed your mind, even if it's not essential? Those things are not random.

Nothing in life is random, and nothing in life is by chance. Take life by the hand and walk with it.

Love it, live it, embrace it, accept it. Don't focus on trying to please other people, including your religious beliefs or their leaders imposing their beliefs on you. Devote more time to self-acceptance, self-love, personal growth, understanding yourself, and forgiving yourself and others, allowing you to transcend what you previously regarded as a mistake.

You must recognize the grace in your life. There are specific tasks you were destined to undertake, ones you were graced to accomplish, and you have some flexibility in this area because God wishes for you to succeed. You were designed for this purpose.

Therefore, rather than focusing on someone else not being meant to do it, they may fail at it. I urge you to move ahead. To assist you, I've allowed you some grace in this aspect so you can glide through it, enabling you to achieve what you need and reach the destination I envision for you.

Once you understand that, you have the grace for this path and journey, no matter what you go through, experience, or do. Let's ensure this is foolproof. You're not entitled to be a criminal. And when I say criminal, you are not graced to kill people; you are not graced to rob people.

Engaging in self-defense or responding to a violation may justify your actions as self-protection. However, this does not give you the freedom to commit acts of terrorism, violence, or hatred indiscriminately. You are meant for love, purpose, and to live your life to its fullest potential. Your choices should reflect your preferences, dislikes, aspirations, and the efforts you're prepared to make.

Chapter 8: The Spiritual Paradox Theory

The following two chapters are essential for helping you recognize patterns and implement the necessary changes to achieve your desired state in life. In spiritual human behavior, the spiritual paradox theory of the soul illustrates two similar concepts, yet possesses different narratives. The accompanying details set them apart in determining what is meaningful in your life.

This theory is unique and specific in several ways. It's similar to differentiating between genuine gold and gold plating. The narrative doesn't suggest that what isn't real for you is not real for someone else. It indicates that you recognize what truly belongs to you versus what might only seem like it does, as the two can sometimes look alike.

They might possess very similar narratives but lack the necessary key components to be the same. This differentiation is essential for identifying what is truly for you and what isn't, allowing you to engage with it effectively.

Much of this arises from deep, meaningful conversations focused on self-understanding, recognizing others, identifying what is helpful or harmful to you, and communicating the value of things. Following this, adapt your patterns and behaviors accordingly.

Your "break-every-chain moment" is about identifying the things, people, and environment you need to change. It is not about changing others since you cannot change a person. Focus instead on cultivating relationships with those who support your growth and align with your aspirations.

This does not mean that those people are beneficial to you at this moment. The preference should be to have somebody as beneficial to you as you are to them. It's not like you'll gain a lot from being around them. And it's not like they will gain much from being around you.

If you complement each other in the right way, if the environment supports both correctly, if the business aligns with your needs, if this ideal reflects your purpose and self-understanding while fostering self-love, then you realize there are choices you no longer need to keep making, as you've become accustomed to them. Life can be tailored based on what is good for you, considering your preferences, aversions, and everything in between.

Understanding your dislikes is often more crucial than recognizing your likes. The things that repulse you, that you find disreputable, or detest all play a significant role in shaping your life. Your decisions about what to avoid influence your direction more than those you actively pursue. By steering clear of certain experiences, you distance yourself from specific places, individuals, conversations, and ways of thinking. When you choose to reject negativity and identify a paradoxical situation, you can lean toward either pessimism or optimism or seek a balance that reflects your true self in every context you encounter.

You can maintain your identity regardless of your circumstances. Thus, you can depend on and have faith in yourself, irrespective of your situation. Unlike the spiritual paradox theory, the idea of the soul focuses on your self-discovery journey as you create the map, which serves as the key to your unique divine life.

While on this journey, the paradox theory intersects with the Deja vu theory, highlighting how to know when to make changes while being where you're meant to be. It explains how to recognize confirmation in nature and surroundings, in what you see and perceive from your perspective. Because of this, you need to alter your thought process; you must change how you think and understand why you think the way you do. This understanding will help you learn and adapt to how you wish to experience life.

For instance, if you wish to view life differently but haven't adopted that mindset or grown up in a negative environment, your default perspective may lean towards negativity. It's essential to surround yourself with individuals who guide you toward a more positive outlook, who offer encouragement, and who will support you as you work to shift your perspective. You'll need to internalize these lessons to foster self-affirmation, ensuring you don't become reliant on others for validation.

The spiritual paradox theory's foundation pertains to the soul's paradox. Typically, this arises during encounters that can change the course of your life. You may encounter a parallel or an intersection of universes.

Every time you meet someone new, your universe intersects with another's, creating a counter to someone else's experiences. Each new meeting represents your universe engaging with someone else's universe. If those two universes collide positively, then wonderful things can happen.

If your universe encounters one that is misaligned, incompatible, or disharmonious with it, chaos may ensue, leading to more problems. The core of the paradox lies in realizing what truly resonates with you versus what merely seems to fit. Certain things are genuinely designed for you in particular ways, shapes, and forms. On the other hand, some elements may not be correct for you in some respects, yet they can still provide enjoyment. However, this enjoyment doesn't imply they hold the same significance. It's essential to learn how to navigate the universe's paradoxes.

The paradox occurs when those two parallel universes intersect, creating something different.

Whenever you encounter someone who makes you uncomfortable or you're not used to being around, you are introduced to a new universe where a paradox may exist. You may meet two people who are the same, but differences in the details create the paradox. This concept is essential in dealing with people and often applies to relationships.

This also involves choosing a home, a job, a thought process, and deciding who to have children with and how to raise them; it determines everything near and dear to your heart. In one split decision, everything could change. One encounter can alter your path completely; for instance, you could be on your way somewhere and make a pit stop, thus missing a life-ending car accident because you didn't go that way.

You might be going about your day or intentionally avoiding someone. If something pulls you to connect with that person, interact, and demonstrate kindness, even before anything else is necessary. This presents a dilemma: Is this someone you are meant to be with, or are they with whom you are meant to create something? While you can easily be with some people, there are specific individuals with whom you can only spend small amounts of time. Occasionally, there are people with whom you can only collaborate on specific endeavors.

The paradox lies in determining who is who and what is what. Here are the steps and tools to help you figure out what's best for you. These insights are based on the information from the previous chapter, incorporating everything we've discussed in this book. At this point, all the information is provided to give you a complete picture of what life can be like, influenced by your thinking patterns and what you dedicate yourself to. It also depends on the information you expose yourself to, including places and perspectives. Remember, you don't always have to visit a location to understand it; do your research, as various tools are available to gather information worldwide. Use that tool to help you understand people.

This paradoxical theory functions as a spiritual evaluation, providing a background check. When you achieve this understanding, spiritual toe-to-line moments arise. How can we assess whether you are in the right position? Is it the right decision, mindset, or ideal to pursue? Some of it involves a process of elimination. The other part is trusting what you know about yourself and how you apply it to everything else around you.

A paradox, by definition, is a seemingly absurd or self-contradictory statement or proposition that, when investigated or explained, may be proven to be well-founded or accurate. The second definition is a statement or proposition that, despite sound or sound reasoning from acceptable premises, leads to a senseless, logically unacceptable, or self-contradictory conclusion. It is a situation, person, or thing that combines contradictory features or qualities. The basis of this definition is that two contradictory things may look the same.

When looking at the definition, the first thought of the pot in the kettle is that you have two pots used to make tea and/or boil water to some extent. They are made differently on the outside but essentially perform the same function. Depending on your teapot or tea kettle, they could be made differently in some way, shape, form, or fashion.

Those two things look different, but are the same. When somebody sees you and judges you based on what they think, without knowing first, that's like the pot in the kettle. That's the paradox.

If you jump into every situation presented to you, thinking it's for you, regardless of the details, then you are setting yourself up for a bad paradox. The paradox concerns close encounters, where the two universes meet, and what you do at that meeting point.

The paradox is for you to figure out what's truly for you and what's not. When you understand what is for you and what's not, along with what you like and dislike, the next step becomes easier. You now know, okay, I've encountered my paradox of life that allows me to reflect, revisit, and ensure that I've grown. If that paradox is met and you are not ready, you will revisit, replay, and recycle everything from before. When you recycle, you repeat everything and return to the same cycle, experiencing the same things again.

Every time you reach that paradox, you will elevate it to a new level or slide back to where you were. One example of a paradox is that you sometimes become thirstier as you drink more water. This can stem from dehydration or an underlying condition, as water quenches thirst.

Understanding the paradox ensures you recognize the consequences of decisions that determine your destination. Based on these consequences, your ability to project possible outcomes will assist you in your paradoxical situations. The paradox theory is derived from encountering things closely, which can shift your life.

Every encounter and sometimes, certain relationships, can shift your life. Make sure you're connecting with the people, relationships, places, things, jobs, and education that can change your life, rather than just doing things to say you're busy or surrounding yourself with people for the sake of having them around. Being open-minded to the paradox means stepping out of your comfort zone.

To shift into a new level and layer of yourself, you must be comfortable with discomfort and leaving your norm. When you accept being outside your norm, you prepare to experience the shift of the paradox. In your normal circumstances, these are the situations and cycles you encounter.

When you encounter these cycles, you interact with this paradox each time you face the same cycle. With every instance, another option becomes available, opening you to the paradox: you can either stay on the same course, continue doing the same things, and keep getting the same results, or you can shift your paradigm and create an entirely new world. Here are some essential things to know.

Exterior things don't reflect interior motives; people can put on acts, present façades, relocate, and engage in actions to alter their identities. People undergo facelifts and various types of plastic surgery, whether it's for breasts, buttocks, noses, ears, or eyes—essentially any procedure that allows for a significant physical transformation. However, spiritually, you are confining yourself to a box if you don't address the issues that trouble you and don't work on healing aspects that facilitate your growth beyond your current state.

You have to be able to take off the bandages, remove all the distractions, and begin to face yourself.

When you confront yourself, the paradox becomes more transparent and more straightforward. You can now see yourself distinctly and say, "Okay, well, in the past, I would have gone this direction because this direction was comfortable. I was accustomed to this direction because it is the one everyone thinks I should take, or is used to me taking."

However, when you pause and make a change, that change can range from minor to significant. Everything transforms once you make the change, and your entire paradigm, perspective, and insight expand with your shift.

To make this shift happen, you must know what exists within yourself, as it depends on where you direct your attention. The paradoxical fabric lets you concentrate on what is best for your soul, your purpose, and how your gift should be expressed. Therefore, as you reflect on the paradox, you must reevaluate yourself and ask, "Okay, so what do I do naturally? What comes without any second thought? What type of people do I connect with naturally? What type of people are detrimental to my personality or my faith? A cancer is just something that seeks to fight you, impede you, and bring you down."

What things are working against your purpose? What things are working against what you want most for your life? If things are not feeding your purpose, they are likely taking away from it and becoming a distraction. The paradox helps you address this and make the necessary shift; to do so, you must recognize that this is the paradox moment—the moment everything changes.

In this moment, when everything changes, as long as you stay focused on your goals, whatever comes your way that does not make sense will shift out of the way. The paradox you attach yourself to, through your actions, thoughts, words, and everything else connected to you, reveals what the universe and God desire for you as you set up your life. What lies behind what you see? Have you conducted the extra detail research necessary to recognize the paradox? This is not something you can specify for yourself; when you reach the paradox, it won't be a matter of it being this or that. The paradox is like when Neo sees the Oracle in the Matrix.

At that moment, if he opts to proceed, he experiences one outcome. However, if he decides to retreat, he encounters a different outcome. It's akin to selecting the blue pill or the green pill; your choice determines whether you delve into the depths of your soul or retreat to the comforts of your familiar past, where you, your family, and everyone else will remain until you choose to discover yourself, love yourself, and understand the direction your soul is urging you towards.

There is something you were put on this earth to do. Spiritual human behavior helps you identify your spiritual gifts, awareness, and intuitive nature, aligning with your purpose. Once we all find our purpose, we contribute uniquely to improve the world.

You will remain trapped in a never-ending cycle until you heal and those around you heal. You will be caught in a cycle of war, hate, self-hatred, and everything else that brings this country and world down. It's important to understand that circumstances can appear one way but also give a false perception of reality.

It's almost like one club in Atlanta. You enter through one door, which appears to be a small area. But if you go through another door, you find an entirely different club. It's as if you wouldn't know about it unless you had been there, as you would never consider that these parts belong to the same building. This scenario perfectly illustrates that, in most places, what you see is not what you get.

There are very few places where you can go beyond the surface level. Then, there's a whole other section, another room—something you didn't even imagine being available or present. You discover what God has for you when you delve deeper. You understand how things might play out by looking beyond the surface level.

Imagine standing before three doors, feeling anxious as you select door number two. The doors offer clues regarding what lies behind each, so you pause to understand the hints before settling on a choice that may not yield the desired outcome. Afterward, you step out and must try again. While you can continue trying, repeated wrong choices can lead to discouragement.

Stepping through the chosen door reveals four more options. Rather than just facing door 123, it is now door 1,234,567.

Instead of having three doors to choose from, your plethora of doors has increased to a point where the decision is more complex because other choices are being presented. But you still have to pick those that enrich your mind and heart.

If you go out and five guys want to date you, you can choose one guy and make your relationship exclusive, going out with him for two or three years. And then guess what? If you realize he's not the right guy, seven other guys might be available instead of just four or five trying to get your attention. Now, there's a tougher choice to make.

To reach a new destination and manifest something different, to get the results you're asking the universe for—results you're praying to God for—you must be willing to stop, look, listen, and pay attention. When you take the time to observe, you can sometimes talk while doing so; you don't have to appear observant to be truly observant.

You don't have to like what it is when you go to a club or are out with friends, whispering to one of them, "Hey, look over there, but don't look obvious." When you're trying to mature and grow and putting in the effort to make changes, you don't have to show that you're changing for those changes to be effective. Sometimes, you may need to appear as if nothing is changing so that no one discourages you on your journey when it does happen.

You can explore various topics, such as your future aspirations, like manifesting ideas. However, there's no need to disclose every detail. For example, when I update on my book, I could share a recent photo, stating, "Hey, I'm about to hit the studio," rather than working productively there. Alternatively, I could snap the picture while working in the studio and share it. You get what I mean? You're in charge of what captures your attention; whatever you nurture flourishes within you. The challenge lies in knowing what to nourish and what to neglect.

Whatever you feed grows; whatever water you give, whatever grass you water grows; whatever water you drink sinks into the things you've planted, soaks into the things you have planted, and helps them manifest. What are you pouring into your expectations? Are you evaluating what you're getting attached to before you commit, ensuring that you aren't recreating the same old situation with just a new person in a new environment, but with the same mindset and behavior patterns?

Now is the moment to heal and grow. Apply everything you've learned to foster your soul's radiance. I'm not referring to a journey to America, but rather to an inward journey of gaining knowledge, achieving understanding, and truly comprehending yourself. This self-awareness equips you to recognize when you're at a paradoxical crossroads. You can either stick with your default reaction or shift your approach, embracing something new and better that fosters your growth and transforms the world. This captures the essence of paradox theory.

It's a soul paradox. It's not based on things that relate to the literal world; instead, it focuses on where things are taking you, how they align with your purpose, etc. This theory involves intersecting parallel or interconnected universes where we meet on this plane. A small change can lead to a significant life transformation: a new wave.

Consider this: Instead of going to the store at 2:30, you go at 2:45. At 235, there was a significant accident. Because you went later, you missed the accident. Missing the accident changed your entire life because now your children can be raised, loved, and cared for by you. Whether or not you realize that that happened, it is not up to you at that moment.

Know that every second brings change. It's like an ever-evolving maze. If you read this book or listen to it through a class, you will have a video of this changing maze.

Each time you make a decision, a part of the maze alters; it can rise or fall, and a wall that wasn't there before may now exist. A decision you made previously can influence something later, as everything you do connects to something in your future.

With every decision, a wall either appears or disappears. When you decide, another door either opens or closes; you multiply or diminish your resources. Each time you make a choice, a shift occurs. Every decision is a pivotal moment in your life. Each day presents a paradox. You either live in a repetitive cycle, experiencing the same thing repeatedly, or you begin to change and approach things in a way you've never considered.

The paradox is being able to recognize spiritually that you're at this thing, at this place, where you see that there is more than one way that can be sought after. You see that there is more than one option available. To determine the path I decide to take, you're either going to go the straight and narrow path you've seen and done before, or I'm going to create a path over this way that may take me through other things. Still, it will get me where I need to be at a different rate, at a different pace, and manifesting things differently.

We are in a different place, at a different pace, and manifesting things differently. That makes the difference: identifying when you can get your triggers together. Then you'll know who you are, self-evaluate, and understand your purpose after realizing that your self has its own will for your life.

Although other people in the world may look like you or think like you, there is only one you on this planet. To be the best you can be, you need to figure yourself out, understand yourself, accept yourself, and love yourself, good, bad, ugly, or indifferent. You take away people's power by knowing and talking about anything someone might use against you. You ensure that you put yourself in a situation where no one can use anything against you.

Once you remove all negative instances of the paradox, it's like taking away all the red pills. If the red pills make you go back to la-la land, you're just lost, and you aren't thinking or trying to get progressively better. It's like throwing away all the red pills for the rest of your life and only having the green ones. Every day, you must wake up and take a green pill to ensure you stay on your path.

As long as you stay on your path and take your green pill, you will be where you need to be. This is hypothetical, but I hope no one has to take a pill every day for the rest of their lives. If you do have to take a pill for the rest of your life, I pray that it transforms your life, shapes your existence, and teaches you something valuable about life. Let go of all the stress in your life so that you can live a calmer, more peaceful, and more productive life.

There is a movie that provides a great demonstration of this. When the person who mentioned this movie told me about it, I didn't know what they were thinking. But when I watched this movie and reflected on it, it was a good example of this understanding, not the nature of the affair in the movie, sliding glass doors.

When I watched the movie, I realized the potential for significance in each moment and each action. I understood how life can be vastly different yet seem the same due to just one small change, one minor correction, or one little difference in direction; this could lead to a completely different outcome.

Some aspects of my life would remain the same if I had never gone to the military. However, other aspects of my life would be different. I would still be me, but how I express my identity would depend on my decisions outside of those that align with my current situation. Therefore, making one decision differently can change your entire life. For example, if you've been married before and have children with your ex-spouse, and now you are divorced, wishing you had never met them means wishing you had never had your children.

If you're happy about your children, you recognize that meeting their other parent was a significant part of your journey that led you to where you are meant to be. You can release any lingering bitterness and continue moving forward with grace. It's all about pinpointing that one aspect that could transform your life.

Instead of thinking you have regrets or things you don't understand, recognize where you are, why, and how you got there. So when you encounter that instance of paradox, and it's time to make that shift, you can make that shift knowing that the last time you chose that, and this time I'm choosing this not based on trying to get somewhere based on someone else's views, but on the needs that you recognize. These are the things you know will work for you. You must adjust these things to get where you're trying to be.

These are the keys to helping you understand and identify the paradox.

Consider all joint supplies, differentiating between people's positions and relationships in your life, or categorizing relationships according to purpose. Based on all joint supply, do those people contribute to your life? Can you nourish them as they nourish you? Can they assist you as you assist them? It's not about whether they can help you, but rather about being equally yoked and meeting you where you are.

The only situation in which I recommend being around individuals who cannot match your level is when you are assisting those who constantly lean on and take from you. These are individuals you are guiding on their journey of growth. They may not be intended as friends. In contrast, those who can provide you with constructive feedback—and whom you can likewise correct—are in a different category.

Those people who can correct you, and whom you can also correct, sharpen one another like iron sharpens iron. These people stand apart from those who can only take from you and take more than they give. When you can recognize this, it will help you immensely.

Additionally, understanding this will assist you when encountering and engaging with people from different backgrounds and narratives. Before you say yes, maybe, or no, and before you commit in ways others think you should, it's essential to see how they fit into God's plan for your life. Ensuring that these considerations align with the path your divine guidance is leading you on is crucial. As I mentioned before, there is an illusion that the grass is always greener on one side than on the other.

Wherever you maintain the grass, it will grow. If you plant seeds, water the seeds, keep the grass cut, and pick the weeds, the grass will grow. Now, this does not apply only if you have artificial grass. If you have artificial grass, it's only for show, and deep down inside, you will see the difference and understand the divine connection of what's for you.

The spiritual paradox involves understanding what is meant for you and what is not, and recognizing where you are, where you desire to be, and how to get there. By utilizing these skills and theories, you can apply knowledge, insight, and perspective to make changes that yield the desired results and manifest the things you desire. Thus, the illusion of the grass being greener is based on maintenance. Even if you buy artificial grass, it costs significantly more.

You may not maintain it weekly, but you will spend much more covering a larger land area. This presents two contradictory elements that don't seem to make sense. It's like encountering two entirely different people who have never met, yet share similarities in nature.

That's something to view as synchronicity. It makes one wonder why they keep encountering these types of people. Is it something they are supposed to learn, a way to assist others, or a way for those people to help them see, do, or envision more purposefully? Understanding what relates to the paradox theory is essential because when faced with two paths, choosing the one that appears most pleasant may reveal that it is not as enjoyable as it seemed.

You may skip over a more rugged path, but it offers more prosperity, light, and grace; it was made for someone to travel on. And there's nothing to slow you down on that path. But you must be yourself and go beyond what you can see.

Think about Oprah for a moment, transitioning from being an underpaid anchorwoman at a news station, where a man told her that not having a family meant she didn't need more money. Now she is one of the wealthiest women in the world, certainly in the US. That's a soul paradox because her soul sees something beyond what her outer appearance suggests. Her soul perceives something more profound than what people saw in her.

Finding alignment empowered her to aim higher than what others perceived and pursue greater ambitions. This process teaches you to identify the right moment to make a change, to recognize when to break free from old patterns and traditions. Doing so opens the door to the evolution and transformations you desire in all aspects of life—physically, spiritually, financially, mentally, and in every conceivable way you could hope for. Consider the seemingly absurd aspirations; the reality is, these ambitious goals can feel unbelievable simply because of their audacity.

Logically unacceptable behavior exists regarding societal norms. Some things are deemed acceptable for men but not for women, and vice versa. For instance, men are often expected to suppress emotional vulnerability, while emotional expressiveness may be more accepted for women. Conversely, it is generally viewed as more acceptable for men to be sexually active at a younger age and to engage in promiscuity compared to women.

If a woman sleeps around a lot, she's called a slut, a whore, and other harsh names. But if a man does it, he's seen as a desirable figure—he's the man, the G, the homie, a ladies' man, and seems to have everything everyone wants. However, that doesn't mean he is happy. Just because someone is a ladies' man and has many partners doesn't guarantee their happiness. True happiness comes from within, and having many partners could be a cover-up for more profound unhappiness.

The goal is to ensure that, no matter who is around or who is not, you are at peace with yourself, your soul, and your journey—the journey God aligned you for. So, when you think about double standards, the paradox arises.

Life would change if double standards did not exist; it would create a consistent standard for women who are supposed to sleep around with men who are also expected to do the same. If you choose to sleep around, it's important to let others know what you are about and where your mind is. If that's your choice, I'm not saying there's anything wrong with sleeping around.

Ultimately, our desires in life shape our willingness to take specific actions. It's essential to recognize what is beneficial for you and what you aspire to achieve, and actively cultivate those aspects, nurturing your wish to flourish.

If you want a lush lawn, you'll start by planting seeds. If you desire an abundance of fish, you would acquire them and provide them with suitable food, akin to planting seeds. Even for fish to reproduce, they need a form of seed. Hence, you must care for what you aspire to nurture.

Society may label a woman who has multiple partners as promiscuous, yet a man in that same scenario is often viewed as more esteemed, almost a hero. While engaging in sexual relations on the first date enhances a man's status, it diminishes a woman's reputation in the eyes of many. The double standard persists: a man's first-date intimacy solidifies his masculinity, while for a woman, it equates to promiscuity.

Having multiple children with different partners is perfectly acceptable. However, when a woman has numerous baby fathers, it often raises concerns, especially if she has too many kids. On the other hand, when a man does the same, he's seen as building a 'kingdom,' and he takes pride in having many children. This highlights the stereotypes that contradict parenting and its challenges in people's perceptions. Having several co-parents, even if they cannot all be present at events or in a traditional marriage, can ultimately strengthen the family dynamic.

A paradoxical shift must occur: if you can have children with multiple women, then you should also be able to marry all of them and support them, especially if children are involved. The idea of being able to father children with various women but not being able to marry them is the paradoxical shift we need to recognize, not only in our individual lives but also within the broader context of society. This shift, which ties into the paradox theory, is a foundation for our destinies.

Such paradoxes are essential for enacting societal change. Certain fundamental aspects of life remain with us forever. If you've watched the movie Inside Out, you understand that core values—shaped by our formative memories and experiences—are lasting.

It is crucial that you learn to address and deal with your problems and emotions properly and manage the various levels of self-control related to your mind, body, habits, and environments while living freely and trusting God. The key is identifying your core issues and allowing those issues to either be transformed by the paradoxical shift or to be maintained and sculpted through it.

When building with people and handling interpersonal relationships, the most critical aspect is ensuring you don't tap into the paradox by mixing your relationships with the wrong people, which means going too far with specific individuals. Some people aren't meant to be with you at the same level or depth as others. Some people are only meant to accompany you to a certain extent.

Some people are not meant to experience everything God has called for them. Identifying the paradox in your own life—and recognizing where a shift or change needs to happen—means understanding what is meant for you and what is not. When I mention gold and gold plated, I'm talking about what you value in life.

Some people get permanent grills, and some get pull-out grills. While both are grills, one stays in place permanently and never comes off, leaving the rotting teeth beneath constantly exposed, while the other can be worn whenever you choose to use it; it's not real, but you can still wear it. Neither option is wrong or inferior to the other. It's based on your preference, what you like, what you desire, and what you wish to bring into your life. You determine what's suitable for your life.

You decide based on your preferences, from a place of healing rather than victimhood, by knowing what you want for yourself, and being confident in your desires. This enables you to make necessary adjustments to achieve your life goals. Change the pattern of your life by recognizing when you have encountered the paradox before the cycle begins again. For more tips on discovering the paradox, please refer to the chapter on the hold-up theory, where you will find more information about red flags and distractions.

Chapter 9: The Déjà vu Theory

The Deja Vu Theory is closely connected to the Paradox Theory; recognizing a paradox often leads to feelings of Deja Vu. The Deja Vu mentioned in the Paradox Theory signals that you have been in this situation before.

Experiencing this can bring frustration and anxiety as you repeatedly encounter the same circumstances without any change. This theory typically surfaces within the paradox when you are prepared to initiate change. When growth is on the horizon, it's essential to acknowledge that personal improvement requires effort.

As you grow, you understand that you are the only one who can nurture your spiritual development. The convergence of the Deja Vu Theory and the Spiritual Paradox Theory indicates a readiness for transformation.

When it's time for the shift, you will keep reliving the same experiences. This can take many forms. For some people, reliving the same experiences means adapting to patterns that distract them or lead them to accept less than what they desire for themselves, what they deserve, and where their goals intend to move.

To understand where the Paradox Theory and the Deja Vu Theory intersect, you must understand the frustration of wanting to improve yet not seeing progress. You must recognize the disappointment of working harder without achieving results. Sometimes, progress is found in your mindset.

Progress can also arise from changing one small aspect, creating a new life cycle for yourself, instead of experiencing Deja Vu, which induces the Groundhog Day effect, where you live the same day repeatedly for 60 to 70 years, leading to a lack of new experiences.

That's 40 to 80 hours of work every week, time spent exercising weekly, and everything except learning about yourself. So you work 60 hours a week, commuting, working, eating lunch, and returning home. Now, let's say you desire religious solitude within a church on Sunday for two or three hours; if you volunteer or attend more than one service, it totals five hours, which includes getting ready for church, driving there, returning, and getting undressed.

That's 65 hours of your time, and then you have to sleep eight hours a day, which amounts to 56 hours a week. If you're doing all these things and are also a parent, you must figure out how to incorporate change.

This represents the first type of Deja vu, and I wish to clarify how Deja vu intertwines with paradox theories, creating a dynamic environment for change and transformation. At the core of this chapter is the concept of Deja vu and the ability to craft new lifestyles by recognizing patterns, which will aid you in navigating life's challenges. However, you are not faced with a conventional test.

There is no examination regarding your character, spirituality, or finances. These aspects may escape your awareness until you grasp their significance. You might doubt their existence because you've overlooked them for so long, yet this does not mean the test and the context in which you live are not fundamental to your struggles and success.

Many individuals encounter challenges but resist confronting them, leading them to revert to familiar patterns. This regression keeps them trapped in a repetitive cycle, going in circles until they finally overcome that challenge. People adopt various distractions and temporary fixes to manage life's pressures.

Some quick fixes won't help you break free from the cycles you know well. This could be a generational pattern in your family's traits, behaviors, dependencies, or a longstanding family characteristic. You need to change this or take other necessary actions to prevent this cycle from repeating, not just in your life but also within your family, especially if it's generational.

This means it affects your life, your children's lives, and if they don't stop it and change it, their children's lives, and so on. You must recognize the generational cycles associated with your family, including health, mentality, habits, temperament, addictions, and the likelihood of effective parenting. As discussed in previous chapters, you need to understand how these factors have shaped you and use that knowledge to develop your purpose at this life stage and impact your children.

Déjà vu is a sequence of events you feel you have seen before or experienced. It can originate from a dream, a day vision, or something you imagine becoming a reality that you envisioned coming to pass. Take a moment, close your eyes, and envision where you see yourself in the next two years.

What do you aspire to achieve in the next two years? Imagine realizing those goals. If raising your credit score is your target, picture yourself with a higher credit score. If you want a new car, picture yourself driving it. If homeownership is your dream, visualize yourself as a homeowner. If you want to be a better parent, imagine yourself fulfilling that role. If you plan to start a family, picture yourself preparing for parenthood with your future partner for the next 18 years.

If your goal is to find love, remember that love is not something you can control. Instead of focusing on a specific person or place, envision love itself. You can visualize a general setting, but avoid picturing a particular person since you can't dictate someone else's feelings. Think about experiences and how you want them to impact you emotionally.

If you want to be on vacation in five years, envision it. Take a moment to see yourself as you would like to be. If you would like to be on a beach, imagine yourself sitting on the sand with the ocean waves before you.

If you need to take a second to find some ocean music, go ahead and find some to envision what it would be like. This is one of the reasons we suggest a vision board: with a vision board, you picture yourself. You picture the words that describe you in all those things.

This vision process and envisioning are meant to help you learn how to meditate, take a moment to breathe, see where you want to be, and then ask God how to get there, which is essential. You need to see yourself as a whole. You must envision yourself being happy and figure out what makes you happy. Then, you can believe it, achieve it, and become it.

Whatever it is you see yourself doing, as long as it's not illegal, and as long as it doesn't force anybody to act against their will or hurt anyone, which is also illegal. Even though it's not illegal to cause emotional pain, you should not want to hurt someone emotionally in any way, shape, form, or fashion.

Envision how you would like your life to go more regularly. Get used to it so that when it happens, you can say, "I saw that coming because I envisioned myself accomplishing this thing."

Deja vu comes in multiple forms.

It presents itself as a paradox. Yet, it also arises from envisioning and dreaming, prompting a sensation within you that suggests, you know, this feels familiar. The core of the matter is recognizing what that familiar feeling means. Unlike in movies, where a machine is used to transcend, in reality, it requires perceiving an environment, a place, a building, and visualizing yourself there before actually experiencing that moment, as if in a parallel universe. Some people prefer to think that their dream state symbolizes a parallel universe.

Spiritual human behavior teaches that your mind acts as a portal, similar to what you see in the movie with Denzel and Paula. This chapter will help you understand the envisioning exercise you did, picturing different goals. Utilize your mind in whatever narrative you've experienced in Deja vu.

In the reality of being a soul inhabiting a body, having a human experience makes our existence encompass two realms. There is what our mind perceives, sees, and discovers about who we are through upbringing and life experiences, along with what it receives from within our hearts; the narrative of our hearts represents our purpose about who God created us to be.

Your mind acts as a bridge linking your heart and body. Your heart, body, and mind create a connection rooted in the mind. The mind directs the body's feelings, interpreting and translating the heart's sensations into physical experiences. Sometimes, the mind can operate in a dream state, like an alternate reality. Learning to access this dream state to connect with God's complete spirit and utilize your imagination to explore different life paths can guide you toward achieving your goals. This process is often instinctual.

There are different types of Deja vu and various forms of it. In this specific type of Deja vu, which relates to the paradox theory, you will use your mind to forecast your path based on the paradox, the situation at hand, the people you involve yourself with, and the possibilities that may arise.

What you see in front of you, what's available to you, the options, and your decisions—whether plan A, plan B, or plan C—do not necessarily have to be distinct. Plan B could serve as an alternative way to make Plan A work. Plan C could be another strategy that builds on what you did in Plan B to enable Plan A's success. It may simply involve another tweak.

The entire alphabet could serve as a better way to enhance plan A. However, what will you do when faced with a choice or dilemma that requires you to consider where this will lead you? I encourage you to use your mind as a tool to envision the possibilities. For instance, what would it be like to have children if I married this person? What are their beliefs? What challenges do they face? What genetic traits might they pass on? What will they contribute to your lives? And yes, if you're a man listening to this, women often consider whether they can be with you. If they like you, they already have plans for you before any relationship progresses.

I recommend not only using this to envision relationships but also for your personal goals. Connect with your innermost self. As you contemplate rapping, school, or starting a business, picture what each of these paths entails. Although all may ultimately return you to business, one might be the journey you are meant to pursue.

Every entrepreneurial journey begins uniquely. Some ventures may start with a singular focus and then evolve, combining various experiences that lead to a specific destination. Therefore, visualize yourself, strategize your life, and consider how you will shape your future so that you will understand the positive, negative, and neutral aspects when challenges arise.

This will help you change the cycles and pass any test that presents a challenge because you are pre-planning. In the Bible, this is called counting the costs. It's called knowing what you are getting into before doing it. Whether you are dating someone new, starting a business, moving to a new place, or taking a new job, whatever you see yourself doing, envision where it can go. Envision the possibilities, the good, the bad, and the indifferent.

Once you can envision all of these things, it will help you make better decisions for your life. What does this have to do with Déjà vu? To catch the paradox, you must discern, know, and relate to when something repeats itself in a déjà vu-cycled manner, offering you a life test. You may continue to date different people, but if they all act precisely the same, you're dating the same person in a different body.

So what we're trying to do now is help you understand how to project your thoughts. Do not project your thoughts or feelings onto someone; instead, establish a framework in which you envision how life will unfold—good, bad, or indifferent. Create a scenario for each possibility in your mind so you can effectively handle and process whatever arises from your choices and decisions.

This involves balancing your feelings, recognizing your emotions, and understanding your desired outcomes. This is when you experience that paradoxical shift. When it's time for this paradox, déjà vu will strike, and you will continue to feel the same, wondering, "Why are you experiencing this? What is happening?"

You need to take charge and instigate these changes to alter the cycle in your life. Your life patterns may be unique, distinct from anything you've encountered or that your family has faced. Beyond your family's experiences, you bear your responsibilities, obligations, and significant events that you must manage, alongside any karma and generational cycles linked to your lineage. Fulfilling personal assignments is essential, and specific challenges related to your identity must be overcome.

Understanding the Deja vu cycle of each guy you've dated seems like this: every place you visit and everyone you meet reflects this pattern. Every friend you have likely fits this mold. If you repeatedly experience negative outcomes, taking a step back and assessing your behavior is essential. Reflect on yourself.

If you aren't always in a negative frame of mind, others might sometimes rely on you to absorb their negative energy. This can lead to friendships with energy vampires, draining your energy. It often feels like a constant struggle, and you may need to distance yourself from these individuals.

You should carefully evaluate the individuals you associate with and devote additional time to complete the project. If this person has lived with these experiences throughout their life, they have the potential to change. However, if they do not transform, will you accept that? The objective is to feel at ease with their authentic self, so even if they remain unchanged, they are still comfortable with that.

Now, envisioning can help you with that. If some people base their decisions on examining the likelihood of success, compatibility, and the chances of achieving their goals, then some decisions would be made differently.

After listening to a young woman discuss her previous habit of overspending on non-essential items. She emphasized the importance of investing money thoughtfully. It was refreshing to hear her share similar views on making meaningful investments and avoiding the waste of money on insignificant items that could eventually be sold, given away, or thrown out. The ability to reflect is indeed precious for everyone.

Learning what works for you and how to make that shift. There was a juncture where she had to decide: Will I keep doing this, or will I pursue a new outcome? Her life has completely turned around since then. She has taken herself more seriously and elevated her money and self-worth by figuring out what she wants to do with her life and making it happen. She envisioned what she intended to do, desired what she wanted, and was willing to work to bring it to life.

For a long time, I have dreamed of writing books. Many of my visions are now becoming reality, which feels like Déjà vu. There were countless moments when I recorded my thoughts, feelings, and goals, and now I can look back and see, "Wow, I predicted that, and I made it happen." I placed it on my vision board, and now it is accomplished. I had that idea there, and look what transpired. I built that on the app, and look what followed.

All these elements manifested in my life because I have tried to imagine myself breaking free from cycles. I've visualized the challenges that might arise from my choices and considered all conceivable narratives, deciding to take a different path to reach my desired destination for myself and my children.

Déjà vu comes in two forms: the personal experience of déjà vu and the second being within somebody else's déjà vu as a third party. Déjà vu simultaneously reflects time, space, and events as a soul growth checkpoint.

Whenever you feel that you've encountered something before—in another realm, a dream, or from a different perspective—you should treat that as confirmation that you are exactly where you need to be. The strength of the Déjà vu experience might inspire you to follow a direction or path you have contemplated. The emotions linked to Déjà vu will guide you toward your actual destination. Likewise, if you experience an eerie feeling, unease, or doubt, it's best to stay away or evaluate further before proceeding. If you feel anxious, be cautious and reassess the situation. If you are happy or excited, go ahead and enjoy.

Even when you feel happy or excited about something, take a moment to process your emotions. Ask yourself, What makes you happy? Then, consider what causes anxiety, fear, or unease. This is crucial because whatever you find that makes you fearful, happy, anxious, or any feeling you're experiencing can connect to healing or aspects you've already overcome and learned from throughout life's challenges. Understanding your feelings, addressing your emotions, and recognizing the connections between them is essential. If you experience anxiety, try to pinpoint the triggers behind it.

If this relates to a childhood trauma, it's essential to revisit it to begin healing mentally. How does revisiting a memory facilitate healing? Why might it evoke anger, sadness, shame, or anxiety? In interactions with others, what aspects of those experiences reflect your accountability? It's essential to recognize that not every experience falls within our realm of responsibility. However, we must still acknowledge our contributions to these situations.

Being accountable for your actions, words, or appearance doesn't mean you're wrong for recognizing the influences that led to any negative, positive, unpleasant, joyful, or complex emotional experiences. Understanding the causes of those feelings is essential. If you want to experience those emotions again or gain new insights, identifying the reasons behind your emotional responses is crucial.

We encourage you not to project emotions from past negative experiences onto new situations, especially when those situations lack similar context. It's important to avoid using past pain as your sole reference point and to make room for fresh experiences. If you've been hurt in a particular area and find yourself reminded of that pain, it's crucial to recognize that these reminders may arise from your discomfort with vulnerability.

This can be a form of Déjà vu because you are triggered to think of that experience in your mind and heart. Every time you reach this area, you feel you will have the same experience and continue to get the same result. This is where the paradox meets Déjà vu in this form because you must take a second and evaluate.

Regardless of how you feel, you evaluate further. It's like a verification process. You verify what you believe, check what you think you know, and re-verify it to ensure that the status and standard you believe in remain consistent throughout your engagement with it, healing it, or flourishing in it.

Sometimes, we rekindle an experience in our minds and reject new experiences from God, thinking they are the same thing. We hesitate to face that again because it caused pain the last time. And if it caused pain previously, it will hurt worse this time since we fell for it again, despite already knowing the outcome from before.

The goal is to learn to trust your instincts, understand your feelings, and explore why you feel this way. Is there anything you can do to change your feelings? If you could alter the outcome, how would it make you feel? If you wish to approach a situation differently, adjust the outcome in your mind and revise the narrative. How did you survive? What insights did you gain? How can you avoid repeating that experience by verifying, researching, deepening your understanding, and asking more questions when opportunities arise?

Be confident in whatever you feel and decide to do, knowing that there are no mistakes you can make moving forward that will stop you from being on your path within God's will for your life. Even if you were to make a "mistake" based on what people think you should do, it could be exactly what God needed you to experience so that you could move forward more mightily. But oftentimes, we are afraid.

Everything in this book comes from applying these things to my life. It took me several years to write and edit this book so that I could ensure that everything in it was verified and solid, so that you could build based on what has helped numerous people build and become better.

You must be able to trust yourself and build that trust by following through on what you want to do. You learn to go with your feelings, listen to your gut, or reevaluate how to assess situations. If something makes you feel bad and you continue to engage in it, leading to a negative outcome, then you realize that the next time you encounter a similar situation, this is your cycle and test.

If you feel trapped in a repetitive cycle, change your habits, embrace new experiences, and advance by shifting your patterns and breaking the cycle. This progression brings you to various levels and layers.

Your goal is to determine where you stand with your ultimate desires.

Complete the vision board process in the next chapter and ask God to show you where He needs you to be.

Trust in your heart and follow the guidance of your soul's purpose, which exists within you and communicates with your brain. This connection aids in managing your thoughts, controlling your movements and speech, and encompasses everything that defines your humanity. Your soul resides within you to fulfill your purpose through this human body.

If the moment calls for birthing something new, a new experience, allow it to. Allow yourself to be confident in the path you are designated to go. And that does not mean you'll have Deja vu every day or every month.

It means that periodically in your life, as you travel the course that God predestined for you, you fulfill your calling and contribute to the bigger picture vision of being on this planet. Use those experiences to begin seeing Deja vu as the confirmation you need to guide you. It may be three or four months, or perhaps a year. That does not mean you are off the path; you could be building towards that moment of Deja vu.

All of these elements could lead to that moment. Depending on the Deja vu you experience, it will indicate how long it has to unfold. However, in the next chapter, we will explore the different ways dreams affect Deja vu.

This confirmation typically happens, particularly when it's merely Deja vu and lacks unsettling emotions. You may recognize having seen this before, which often reassures you that you're on the correct path since you've encountered it previously.

You are revisiting something that has already occurred. As long as no negative feelings are involved, you can move forward with confidence, receiving the grace to achieve what's meant to come next. Chapter 10 discusses alignment theory and provides insights into signs, dreams, how the universe communicates, Deja vu, precognition, and premonition.

One goal of Deja vu is to use Deja vu moments to reflect on and break recognizable cycles within one's individual life and family structure. Now, in relation to cycles, everything is based on patterns.

You possess various patterns: family dynamics, environmental influences, social behaviors, learned responses, survival strategies, and healing patterns. Understanding spiritual human behavior enables you to recognize the patterns in your life that you've become familiar with and to identify the necessary steps to address the unhealthy vulnerabilities you observe.

This process enables you to start developing new, healed, healthy, and balanced patterns that reflect your desires, the actions you wish to pursue, and what you believe will benefit you in the long run. Patterns can also be referred to as generational curses and traditions, a topic we discussed earlier.

Karma follows a patterned system. It is based on cycles of behavior in which you actively engage. If you put out negativity, negativity will return to you. The more positivity you share, the more positivity will come back to you. Furthermore, karma can manifest as a direct consequence of your actions, or it may become generational, where your behavior persists for so long that you remain uncorrected, leading to lessons being passed down to your child instead. Your behavioral patterns can influence your child, who may then replicate the actions you've always taken. In such cases, your child may be unable to evade karma's lessons.

Those are karmic laws that exist. Even if you learn later in life, if you never teach your child what you learn, guess what? That generational lesson will carry on. It's not necessarily a curse if you learn a lesson and break that cycle to create a new pattern for your or your children's lives.

Karma is another term for patterned behavior because there will be an effect if you continue to act this way. Every time you behave like this, it has a consequence. Therefore, you are training yourself to break traditional bad habits and practices that result in adverse outcomes or results that are not as positive as you would like them to be.

If you fail to learn a lesson or absorb specific experiences, you can still guide your child or any young person toward a better path by sharing your insights. You are changing the karmic pattern in your family or life situation. Even if you've made mistakes, faced challenges, or dealt with karmic energies from any source, taking responsibility for those lessons is essential to make amends. Depending on your actions, Karma will only impact you as much as you permit.

What are you actively engaging in? What patterns do you observe in your life today? What recurring behaviors do you notice? Are you frequently engaged in conflicts or arguments? Do you find yourself in similar types of relationships repeatedly? Are you constantly moving from one place to another, or do you keep allowing people into your life who inflict emotional harm or disregard how they treat you, particularly when you treat them with more care?

What patterns have you learned from your environment? The patterns you exhibit are those you engage in repeatedly; they may not have originated from a relative or have a specific onset, but you find yourself doing them consistently. These individual patterns may have become the key factors for your survival.

We will explain survival patterns. Individual patterns represent your daily activities. What do you do consistently? Some individuals develop distinct patterns based on their personalities.

You will likely make greater progress if you align your life patterns with your goals and personality. This customization allows you to tailor your life according to your preferences and self-awareness. As a concept we explore in spiritual human behavior, this emphasizes the responsibility of your actions viewed through a spiritual lens. You might notice recurring family patterns and face challenges in maintaining a strong marriage. Sometimes, divorce impacts families due to misguided counsel from relatives offering poor advice. Nevertheless, divorce doesn't imply your family is doomed to this fate.

Suppose your family often selects partners that lead to divorce, or infrequently engages in relationships, and you find yourself attracted to the same types of partners. In that case, this may reveal a personal pattern influenced by your standards and environmental lessons. It can also relate to the type of men you choose, or if you're a man and you consistently select a similar type of woman, it could be shaped by the kinds of individuals you have encountered and grown accustomed to being around.

Most people think they like bad boys, but they don't genuinely enjoy them. They are accustomed to a specific nature. They know how to handle themselves in these situations and often possess survival tactics to get by, especially if they come from a background where they had to fend for themselves, like growing up on the streets or being consistently unattended or uncared for.

Environmental patterns may arise from consistently encountering this particular type of environment. In some communities, this behavior often manifests as: killing one another, failing to unite, and competing fiercely. Nowadays, many individuals exhibit negative, bitter behavior patterns because they have spent their entire lives in adverse, bitter environments.

If you were raised in a situation where you constantly face yelling or fussing, or if you're in a city with frequent gun violence, like Chicago or even a smaller place like Dayton, Ohio, that environment influences your behavior. It affects how you navigate not just in that setting, but also impacts your interactions with other environments. Your primary survival instinct becomes about avoiding danger. Similarly, if you have experienced molestation, a key survival strategy involves avoiding circumstances that might lead to another incident like that.

If you have experienced violence, your survival skills may involve learning to fight and avoiding potentially dangerous situations. Sometimes, survival skills can include deceiving others to gain an advantage. These patterns of behavior can become ingrained. For instance, if you grew up resorting to violence or intimidating others as a means of survival, you may come to believe that threatening, harming, or bullying others is necessary to earn respect, affection, or even admiration.

It's been discovered that you can naturally shift away from survival instincts and behaviors by focusing on your personal growth, skills, and discipline. Instead of forcing these survival patterns, they evolve into healthier habits. Social behaviors might include negative comments on social media or frequently going out to clubs, engaging in casual encounters, and being socially active. Conversely, social patterns can also be characterized as antisocial behavior.

Social patterns refer to how you interact with the world around you. Over time, you may learn to balance these patterns as you recognize the types of environmental patterns you possess and the individual personal patterns you exhibit. What kind of family dynamic patterns do you observe? Some people grow up in families where everyone is a side chick or where extramarital affairs are common. Others are raised in families where everyone gets married for the long haul. Remember, patterns aren't always destructive. You are also observing good patterns.

It's essential to recognize damaging patterns, especially in your family dynamics. These patterns can manifest as everyone being excessively invested in others, negatively affecting their well-being. Family members often display extremes of love, care, and adaptability, welcoming many into their lives. Accommodating too many individuals triggers survival instincts. It is vital to be discerning. As a result, people often hold back from bringing new individuals into their lives.

With the mindset that no one is wholly good and everyone can treat you poorly, healing offers a more perceptive viewpoint. Although your initial trust in others may be diminished, the goal should be acknowledging that you start from a place of distrust. However, you have discovered how to foster trust and establish mutual respect, which is no longer an obstacle to your progress.

All of these environmental patterns we observe are those we are exposed to and can learn from. The patterns you learn are the ones that help you adapt most effectively in your life. The patterns arising from all of these factors are learned patterns.

You can create patterns, but you must consciously examine the patterns you learn and determine how to assess what you need to do to move forward and change the patterns you dislike. Not all learned patterns are destructive; some individual patterns you possess are not in survival mode.

You need those because they are part of who you are. Some aspects are not part of family dynamics; they reflect who you are.

Some family dynamic patterns may not be negative. Possessing a strong personality is not a detrimental family dynamic. Characteristics such as a strong will, determination, being a go-getter, and embodying the qualities of a strong alpha individual are not negative traits or patterns.

Maintain positive patterns, recognize those that aren't beneficial in the long run, and establish a balance based on the patterns you embrace. Indeed, good karma is real. It thrives within the positive behaviors and patterns you display.

If you're consistently giving and loving, even if some people take advantage of you, it's a positive pattern to uphold. This is good karma that you're cultivating. Let others choose not to like you for any reason. That has nothing to do with you. It's their issue. How others feel about you and treat you is their responsibility because they have to face that karma.

When you understand karma, instead of being bitter, angry, and hostile, you will begin to speak more positively, allowing you to see more positively. Overall, whatever energy we put out is the energy that develops around us. If you cultivate negative energy with the people around you, that negative energy expands and grows. The more people tap into your negative energy, the more negativity increases.

There is a difference between negative energy and the truth. Many people dislike the truth because it forces them to step up their game. The truth encourages them to do better, be better, and speak better things. It compels them to reflect on themselves in a way that requires self-assessment. When we avoid this, we continue to experience patterns of bad karma.

Bad karma is simply you talking about someone. Now, someone is talking about you. Instead of saying, You know what? That stops here with me. I'm not doing that anymore. I'm not being that. I'm not, you know, continuing to regurgitate negativity; instead of stopping it.

Negativity brings more negativity. We have to know that the karma from our behavior can impact ourselves and other generations. We need to define healed patterns of behavior.

The healed patterns are developed once you've revisited every area of your life that's triggered—everything that caused you to react, everything that caused an emotional response without logical thinking.

Sometimes, even if it's logical thinking, understanding your emotions will help you grow long-term. The ultimate goal is to emotionally process everything you go through and make the necessary changes to achieve your goals. To manifest the life you want, you must be accountable.

You must recognize when patterns need to change. You must understand when Deja vu says, "Hey, I see you, you see me, you're supposed to be here. That's why you feel like you've been here before."

Now keep going down this path.

Section 5:
Looking For A Sign
Understanding Signs and Wonders

Chapter 10. The Alignment Theory

This Alignment Theory focuses on grasping the alignment process and recognizing the signs designed to assist you along the journey.

Upon achieving a level of understanding that comforts you with the Paradox and Déjà vu theories, you are at a plateau toward your desired destination. Having laid your foundation, it's now time to expand. Generally, people seek signs from God for direction and understanding. We will explore the various types of signs, discuss how the universe communicates, and delve into the realm of dreams.

Seeking God's guidance is essential at every stage of life. In various pursuits, individuals often ask God for a sign. However, not everyone understands how to search for, recognize, interpret, and embrace those signs. The core of this alignment theory focuses on being receptive to answers that may be overlooked, since the signs God gives are not always expressed verbally.

These signs could manifest as changes in the environment, actions or words of others rather than direct communication, or divine insights that come to you. It's crucial to recognize that a sign can also be easily observable.

Often, signs present themselves through experiences or encounters. These signs enrich your understanding of your spiritual gifts and life's calling. They will guide you if you remain open to them and know what to look for.

Provision, Faith, and Favor

Provision primarily signifies receiving assistance from God. It can also describe a condition or requirement stated in a legal document, a benefit granted directly by the Pope, or a position. Additionally, provision functions as a verb, meaning to supply food, drink, or equipment, especially for a trip, or to allocate an amount in an organization's account for a recognized liability.

Therefore, it involves creating opportunities for events, making arrangements for specific actions, and altering the context of documents. It encompasses adding, multiplying, and subtracting. In Middle Eastern contexts, it also relates to the idea of foresight, including intuition and similar concepts.

Faith is defined as complete trust or confidence in someone or something; it represents a strong belief in God or the principles of a religion grounded in spiritual understanding rather than proof. Additionally, faith encompasses a system of religious beliefs and deeply held convictions or theories. We will explore the distinctions between these concepts and provide a robust foundation for your faith shortly.

Lastly, *Favor* refers to approval, support, or affinity for someone or something. It represents an act of kindness that goes beyond what is customary. It can also mean to express or demonstrate approval or preference for something. Kindness beyond the norm may indicate favoritism or an inclination toward someone.

Clarifying these definitions is crucial as they are pivotal in spiritual human behavior.

When discussing signs, dreams, and cosmic elements, we must first recognize the nature of our assignment. Our assignment refers to the path that God has set for us. It doesn't need to be particularly profound or mysterious; it simply indicates that our life's journey constitutes our assignment.

Your responsibility encompasses your assignment. If you have children, they are a part of your assignment. Firstly, you must care for yourself, your children, and your household. Following that, your assignment extends to assisting those around you. Recognize that provision arises when you align with the life path God has set for you. For some, this may appear as luck, where things happen effortlessly. This is the provision God, the universe, or the creator has granted in your life.

This concept is also connected to grace. Grace will guide you, while provision directs you toward your intended goals. Therefore, clarifying your objectives is crucial for discovering your vision and aspirations. This insight will help you identify the provisions necessary for your life.

If you find yourself heading in a specific direction and nothing seems to go your way, it may be a sign to reassess your actions, destination, and the company you keep. Making these adjustments could reveal the provision you need. I've learned that when things are meant to unfold, they do so smoothly, as if they were preordained, even if that wasn't the case initially.

You get the job, and soon after, you find the house. Things seem to unfold in your favor one after another. Even if it's not daily, something new continuously arises, while some achievements take time to develop. When you commit to your prayer and meditation, feel guided to take action, and follow through, it simply works out.

Let me provide an example: Slutty Vegan. Pinky launched her business in August 2018 and grew from operating a food truck to establishing a restaurant. She attracts lines that are two to three hours long each day at both locations—the truck and the physical restaurant. She has made remarkable strides in just six months and likely earned millions. This isn't to pry into her finances, but to illustrate how quickly someone can progress from one point to their destiny with determination.

Note: Since the initial writing of this book, Pinky Cole nearly lost Slutty Vegan to investors in 2025 after opening over 11 locations across various states, college campuses, and airports. Fortunately, she repurchased the business and regained sole ownership during restructuring. While some locations temporarily closed, Slutty Vegan continues to thrive under her original leadership.

When I bought my first home, I was advised it was impossible due to my poor credit. Yet, six months later, I signed a contract, and my new home was under construction, with plans to move in seven months later. I want you to understand that by aligning with your faith and letting go of mental barriers, you remove all limitations on your thoughts, intentions, and all aspects of your life.

This means ignoring the expectations others have for you.

It means not trying to impress people you cannot depend on, who do not depend on you, and who are not within your household. Even when trying to impress, it should be by merit and what you do, not by what you have. Provision will guide you if you do not force your way.

Sometimes we appear to be following a path, and then it comes to a halt. This doesn't imply that you are at fault; it simply suggests something else is unfolding. Adjustments are necessary. Actions must be taken. Occasionally, it's essential to pause, as we may not want to exceed the pace intended for our journey.

If you've been called to a purpose and seek alignment, all other tasks you are meant to pursue can also align with you. Alignment encompasses not just your presence in the right place, your communication with God, and your understanding of your mission, but also embracing the grace, time, and favor necessary to guide you toward your true calling.

You'll notice provisions manifesting and doors opening effortlessly as you align yourself. They will swing open without needing you to push, bang, kick, beat, or force them down. If you maintain focus, you will achieve your goals.

Faith involves taking actions that support your declared goals and beliefs. When you assert your faith, it will be evident in everything you do, as all aspects of your life will be grounded in that faith. Your communication, actions, and choices across all areas will reflect your faith and what you say you believe or want to happen.

The Bible states that faith is the essence of what we hope for and the proof of what we cannot see. It is what you cling to, confident that your efforts will contribute to the substance that upholds hope.

By working towards your goals, you can receive what God has intended for you. When you place your faith in God for something, you will actively pursue it. Your determination grows as you work toward it; if it's meant to be, it will be. There will be provision and favor. Favor means having things align in a way that is best for you.

This implies you take initiative. Imagine someone saying, although this isn't the norm, today we're here to assist you in obtaining what you need or what you are trying to accomplish. If you apply for a job and they currently don't have any openings but decide to see if they can create a position for you, that is an example of favor. It starts with your mindset and ability to set your intention for good things to happen and things to work in your favor.

Note: Sometimes, when things don't go as you hoped, it's a blessing. God (The Source of All) knows what lies ahead and may protect you from unseen troubles. Think of your favorite superhero movie, where the hero pauses time to rescue someone in danger quickly.

This illustrates a provision. When events favor you, view them as a sign from God. While some may advise caution, reminding you that the enemy also grants rewards, remember that God blesses anyone who applies the principles of His system. You don't have to be excessively righteous to receive God's blessings; instead, apply these principles to reach your objectives despite how you feel about your current situation.

Here's how the universe conveys messages of alignment to you. These signs are gentle nudges from the universe, reflecting your prayers to stay on your current path or alter your course.

Signs can take many forms. You may find yourself reflecting on an idea when a stranger, especially in the age of social media, shares a post that aligns with your thoughts. This phenomenon indicates that your thoughts connect with others. Furthermore, signs can show up as street signs, license plates, or messages displayed on vehicles while you are contemplating something specific.

For example, if you notice a rainbow while praying, it may be interpreted as a divine sign. According to the Bible, a rainbow represents the promise that life will continue and that a flood will never again destroy the earth. See how that works.

A variety of signs could manifest in your life.

Dreams and Visions

Moreover, signs can manifest in dreams. Dreams consist of imagery that occurs during sleep, but can also happen while awake. Although you might have multiple dreams throughout your sleep cycles, this book focuses on the more vivid ones.

The vivid dreams you recall when you wake up. So, although you may dream about random things throughout the night and recall having different dreams, your most vivid dreams will be the most important. However, the other dreams may be instances of Déjà vu.

You may have some dreams you do not remember in detail, but when you encounter that moment in real life, you'll experience Déjà vu and think, "I've seen this somewhere before." When you recall that you witnessed it in a dream, you will remember that moment from the dream, which will be Déjà vu and a confirmation of being in the right place at the right time by seeing something you previously observed.

Everyone experiences dreams a little differently. Within those dreams, you might discover various ways to research the information in them.

It's suggested that when you have dreams, you should get a notebook or notepad and write them down. The goal of recording those dreams, especially the exceptionally vivid ones you remember, is to help you later if those things happen locally or in distant lands. In my household, we are all known to have dreams, which is very common on my maternal side.

Dreams are commonplace for us and have manifested in reality, even in the lives of others. God may communicate with you through a vision or a strong thought, which, if acted upon, can become crucial. Vision involves the capacity to envision or strategize your future using both imagination and wisdom.

It's a mental image of your future, influenced by experiences from dreams or stances you've come to have. While dreams and visions share similarities, visions can occur while awake. Another way the universe communicates is through daydreams, vivid mental images that distract you from your current focus.

The universe conveys messages through intuitive insights, enabling you to anticipate events before they occur in reality. You are more inclined to have visions, dreams, or intuitive insights, such as daydreams, when you are curious about the present and the future and searching for answers. Visions or dreams can manifest anytime—during the night, naps, or other restful periods.

Writing allows a vision to be understood and automatically expressed. This is one of God's spiritual gifts, which I will discuss in chapter 11.

I want to emphasize the significance of a vision board when it comes to visions. It's a tool that visually illustrates your aspirations. Think of it as a collage of elements you picture for yourself—your goals are visible to inspire their manifestation in reality. A vision board consists of images, magazine cutouts, or anything you feel can become part of your life, continuously displayed to draw these desires towards you.

Messages

Let me explain how the universe conveys messages through your environment. It can introduce animals into your life. Have you ever seen an animal at the right time and thought, "Wow, where did this animal come from?" While some animals might inspire fear, there's no reason to be afraid unless you're in danger.

Maintain your curiosity.

Inquire with God about the significance of the animal's presence. If needed, explore online resources to uncover what this animal symbolizes within the totem pole of life and the spiritual animal realm. Have you ever pondered its meaning? Have you researched whether it is relevant to your current life situation or future encounters with the same animal? Don't simply react with surprise.

Take a moment to observe. Reflect on your thoughts and feelings when you see that animal, as they might serve as confirmation. Then, delve into the spiritual meanings of any animal you encounter that could hold a connection.

The thing is, if we begin looking up all the animals we encounter in the spiritual realm and what those animals signify—whether it's your spirit animal or something trying to convey a message—we might find ourselves baffled by what God is attempting to reveal through the animals that enter our lives. Additionally, we may dream of animals, accidents, heaven, and Earth, and witness many other things.

This chapter encourages you to be open to the messages from God, the universe, and your inner self. The universe communicates through synchronicity, the coincidental occurrence of events that appear linked, despite lacking a clear connection.

When an idea or thought you've had begins to manifest, don't dismiss it as mere coincidence; it's a sign of synchronicity. For example, you might spot a car with the license plate 777 while driving. If the number 777 holds personal meaning for you, consider it a message from God. Likewise, if you encounter something bearing your name, recognize that you would have missed that sign if you hadn't been at that exact moment and location. This is how life unfolds around you.

External factors can shape certain elements. Before continuing, we should address the digital manipulations that seek to influence people's online opinions.

If you understand the algorithm, you can differentiate between signs from God in the universe and the influences of those who communicate messages in plain sight. As you explore these concepts, you will learn to distinguish what constitutes a sign versus merely an aspect of the matrix.

Number Sequences

A number sequence is a series of numbers that share a commonality or imply a spiritual message. As I mentioned earlier, these sequences can appear in patterns, such as 777, 1111, or 111.

Please take note of these number signs as they may indicate the universe is trying to get your attention. Note down what you're thinking about when you encounter them.

Whenever you believe a number might have significance, note what you're doing at that time and observe the events that follow after noticing that number. This practice will aid in remembering its message. Sometimes, you may find yourself contemplating something spiritual and seeking prayer or guidance.

Distractions often arise during these moments. It could be a siren, a horn, driving frustrations, or something falling, pulling your focus away. You then have the choice to try to recollect your thoughts or become sidetracked by these interruptions.

Noticing specific number sequences may simply stem from being more aware of your surroundings. Conduct online research for further details about numbers and angel numbers. When searching digitally, ensure you reference the most commonly discussed themes, as a vast amount of information can sometimes conflict.

It's best to find common ground and, from the similarities, derive results that are easy to understand and apply to your life. Do internet searches and feel excited to discover information.

When you read a book and find something unclear or lacking details, take the time to investigate. During this process, collect all relevant information and examine all search results before choosing what you want to read or listen to.

Start by tuning in to what resonates with you. Then, evaluate opposing viewpoints as well. Consider everything thoroughly.

You need to figure out how to organize this information coherently. Doing so will give you a clearer understanding and perspective on your research. It's crucial to recognize that you'll encounter numerical patterns frequently. Specific number combinations are believed to carry particular meanings.

Conduct your research. From your findings, explore what specific number patterns signify for you. What has significance for others in the research may hold a different meaning for you.

It is advisable to spend time praying, meditating, and seeking guidance from your angels and God about what these experiences mean for you. Now, let's change our perspective. These experiences indicate how God and the universe convey messages to you.

Ignoring Signs & Answered Prayers

Ignoring God leads to a flood of signs. Everything seems to shout for your attention, delivering messages to get your attention, leaving you feeling swamped by the surrounding signals. You may feel adrift or recognize the need for change, yet struggle to implement it. Rest assured, breaking habits can be difficult. Generally, it takes 21 days to develop a new habit.

Whether you've had a habit for 21 years, three months, three years, or seven years, it will likely take some time to break free. However, the simplest way to overcome a habit is to learn new information—either about the habit itself or as a substitute for it. If you have a habit, it is time to replace it with new knowledge and unlearn what you previously understood.

Another important aspect of hearing from God and following your path is that God often communicates with us through a quiet voice deep within our souls. Depending on what resonates with you, this can be described as a gut feeling, intuition, or intuitive insight.

When God communicates with us through words or visions regarding others, locations, or objects, it's essential to take that information and put it into action. By doing so, we create space for God to facilitate the next step in alignment with His guidance. If we struggle to grasp what God is conveying, He may deliver the message through alternative means.

The sequence typically involves God first communicating with you, followed by a sign—this could be an animal, a person, a lyric in a song, or a message on the radio—anything that draws your attention to what you've prayed about, inquired of God, or contemplated on your own, as your intuitive nature begins to guide you toward a message. I want to clarify that I am not trying to be eerie or unsettling; instead, it's intended to help you become more aware of when God is attempting to capture your attention and guide you in a specific direction. After a significant period of ignoring divine prompts, God won't provide different guidance if the answer remains unchanged.

You might feel like you're no longer receiving communication from God because you aren't hearing anything new, seeing new signs, or experiencing fresh circumstances, all due to not fully heeding the last message that touched your spirit.

When you overlook the earlier messages, God may send someone to guide you. This person could be unfamiliar to you, and may not even be the last messenger God intended for you.

Sometimes, God may send someone to serve as a warning before significant events occur, alerting you to the potential consequences of confident choices. It's essential to remain receptive to all signs from God. You may miss important messages if you dismiss those God sends your way. If you are closed off to others, you might overlook opportunities to ask questions or gain more profound insights that could have helped you. Thus, we must stay open to receiving guidance from God in various forms and channels, not solely through our thoughts and spirits, but also in the world surrounding us.

This guides your spiritual nature, as navigating this universe requires knowing you're on the right path. When you pray for God's angels to surround you, those angels will assist you in your pursuits when invoked. If God communicates a message through your thoughts or a sign, and you overlook this sign, He will convey it through another means.

If you still don't understand, God will send someone to reiterate it. Once God communicates, the message remains unchanged. You may remain oblivious until you act on what was previously revealed.

When you miss the opportunities God has placed in your path, He adjusts the plan so you don't overlook them again. It's akin to taking a detour; an alternative route is available if a street is blocked and an event is happening.

We need to determine which route will lead us to our desired outcome. Redirection can occur when our previous direction is misaligned rather than due to incorrect instructions. Often, you must go through specific experiences to grasp essential lessons that guide you to your destined purpose.

Don't view it as a loss if you ever feel like you've missed something. Instead, consider it a lesson essential for guiding you to what is truly meant for you. Once you understand that what is destined for you cannot pass you by, you will be more open to receiving signs from God.

Upon closer examination, we can often observe how our human intelligence is artificially replicated and presented to us, aiming to outsmart the natural order of life and its elements. Many systems rely on search engines, algorithms, and hidden observational methods. Numerous games, surveys, and questionnaires on social media are designed to think on your behalf, gathering insights to make assumptions about your identity.

They want to know your interests and start catering to your thought patterns and processing what you see. Anything you are likely to click on or have shown interest in will appear as an ad or clickbait. Once you begin to do your Google searches or whatever search engine you choose, you will begin to see ads that correlate with the things you find yourself interested in, so that you can be pushed ads and things you like.

When you shop online or in-store using your debit card, it can now monitor your activity and target you with advertisements on social media for products you might be interested in. To be clear, when it comes to dreams, signs, and wonders, time is the only reliable confirmation of what anyone can tell, show, interpret, or believe.

The goal of spiritual human behavior, especially the signs and wonders, dreams, and grasping how the universe communicates, is to assist you in starting to manifest your goals. A key element of this process is understanding what you truly desire. Developing a vision board or positioning your goals in prominent locations helps keep your aspirations at the forefront, constantly reminding you of what you are striving for, aiming to achieve, and working towards accomplishing.

Achieving your goals, dreams, and visions can be challenging. The primary difficulty lies in maintaining focus and avoiding distractions that do not contribute to your objectives. This is where having tunnel vision becomes essential.

You must concentrate solely on your aspirations to attract what you desire into your life. If you pay attention to feelings of hatred, misunderstandings, gossip, or anything else undesirable, you will only attract more of these negative experiences into your life. Breaking free from limitations is essential while maintaining a sense of innocence and childlike faith.

Understanding that you should not be placed in a box as you move forward is essential. You deserve to pursue anything you desire, anything purposeful, and anything that will enhance the love within yourself. You need to explore opportunities.

Exploring new experiences, connecting with yourself, and trying to understand, love, and appreciate who you are is essential. Doing this can liberate you from external pressures about what you can or should do, as only you truly know what is best for you.

If you constantly prioritize others' opinions, you'll remain unaware of what truly serves you, confining yourself to their expectations. Preserving your innocence can be challenging, depending on your life experiences. However, as you heal and your compassion grows, your innocence will naturally evolve with your journey.

Healing is a lengthy journey that calls for understanding the root causes of your pain, rather than fixating on the person responsible for it. It's crucial to reflect on the insights the hurt may provide. Think about whether any lessons exist. In certain instances, especially if you have endured any form of abuse, recognizing those lessons can be particularly difficult. You did not deserve that experience of abuse. It was unnecessary, and the pain and sickness within that person were unjustly directed at you.

Please forgive yourself for allowing it to happen. You are not responsible for what happened, and you should not hold yourself accountable for it. Forgive yourself for being in that situation and ask God, or whoever you worship or pray to, how you can learn and grow from it so it no longer affects you. Childlike faith is a cherished quality; it's a divine gift that encourages openness to imagination.

To nurture this faith, you must embrace the potential of anything you wish for while letting go of what doesn't belong to you. In childhood, you perceive everything in terms of good and evil. As an adult, you can still maintain that openness while learning to adapt to the things that do not serve your purpose, well-being, family, or mental health.

Having a childlike faith means maintaining belief in your goals and purpose, without letting others sway you from what God has revealed. As you read through these chapters, God communicates insights about actions you should take, aspects of yourself you can heal, opportunities for personal growth, and ways to contribute positively to the world. Pay attention to the feelings that arise as you apply what you learned in this book.

If necessary, read it once more. If you have any questions, please email me and my team. If you've strayed from your path, remember that you can always return by making one decision in favor of your goals. When you stay focused, each decision leads to another, aligning perfectly with your intended direction.

Please remember: I can't specify the signs God may provide to affirm your beliefs regarding the path you should pursue; it's up to you to discover them during your meditation and prayer with God.

This chapter section encourages interaction. You will be presented with several questions for your reflection, and you can mentally note your thoughts, use a pen and paper, or take notes on your phone if you don't have a journal.

What is your purpose?
What do you want to accomplish most in life?
List your three top priorities.
What are your five-year goals?
What are your ten-year goals? *Your ten-year and five-year goals should align.
What are your lifetime accomplishment goals?

What do you desire to achieve throughout your lifetime?

How are you progressing towards achieving your goals?
What are the necessary tools that it will take to bring your goals to real life? How would you like to live long-term?
Last question, what would you do if you could do anything without worrying about working or retirement?

If you have dreams, start writing them down. If you have visions, record them. Document everything you experience spiritually to revisit those moments when needed. Take a moment, close your eyes, and imagine where you see yourself in two years.

What would you like to accomplish in the next two years?

Imagine achieving your goals. If it's about improving your credit, visualize better credit. If it's acquiring a new car, picture yourself with that car. If your aim is homeownership, see yourself as a homeowner. If you're working on being a better parent, visualize yourself excelling in that role. If you plan to become a parent, see yourself pregnant and practicing parenting alongside the person you wish to co-parent with for 18 years.

When it comes to love, remember that you can't control it fully. Instead, visualize yourself in love. Avoid focusing on a specific individual; instead, think about the feelings you want to experience, the places you'd explore, and the moments you'd cherish.

Now, take a moment to envisage your dream vacation five years from now. Picture what that trip would look like.

If your ideal vacation spot is a beach, imagine yourself basking in the sun on the sand, with the ocean waves gently lapping at the shore. If you want, take a moment to find some ocean sounds online to help enhance your vision.

This is part of why we advocate for creating a vision board: it allows you to visualize your aspirations. A vision board helps you see yourself embodying the words that represent all your desires and goals.

Section 6. The Commission

Chapter 11: The Lightworker Theory

The Lightworker Theory assists you in recognizing and utilizing your gifts, talents, and skills to support yourself and others in adapting to enlightenment and gaining knowledge, wisdom, and understanding.

This section is titled The Commission because once you learn and apply the theories of spiritual human behavior, you begin to embody each principle and fulfill your purpose. Through this process, you become a guiding light for others, demonstrating how to lead a life of mental liberation and wholeness before connecting with anyone else or inviting additional people into your life.

The theory centers on recognizing and discovering your role within the Great Love Commission. You might wonder what a lightworker is and what the Great Love Commission is. A lightworker has awakened to the truth of love and self-awareness, embracing their calling by utilizing their talents, gifts, and skills to spread enlightenment to others, helping them experience love, peace, and light. The Great Love Commission is the task of spreading Love and Enlightenment worldwide.

A lightworker aims to assist others in becoming authentic versions of themselves. They are not here to lead or dominate anyone, but rather to empower others to take charge of their own lives while guiding them in nurturing their inner light independently. Lightworking involves awakening the soul amid this human experience, helping individuals recognize their purpose on Earth and understand their role as souls.

Spiritual human behavior serves as a guide for lightworkers and those looking to discover their soul purpose. It enables individuals to recognize their inherent gifts, talents, skills, and self-worth. The essence of lightwork is to assist others in becoming their true selves. Being a lightworker isn't a role you apply for; it's about nurturing the light within you and letting it radiate outward. When you begin to shine, you empower others to feel free to shine.

The Great Commission of Love reflects the "each one, teach one" principle. Once you awaken to your purpose, experience self-love, true love, and divine love—topics that we will delve into further—and attain peace and wholeness, your mission is to help others see their value in God's light through the gift of enlightenment.

When you incorporate these theories into your life, they become powerful tools. You will likely want to help others use these theories in ways that fit their needs. Since we all have different backgrounds, ethnicities, and family dynamics, not everyone will interpret each theory in the same way. Each individual has a distinct upbringing and viewpoint, which means that what works for one person may not be effective for another.

These theories can be customized to suit your needs, preferences, and circumstances. This approach focuses on self-reflection instead of trying to psychoanalyze you or assume a therapist's role, allowing you to express yourself freely. As a company, Speaking Freedom seeks to empower you to act with intention while encouraging others to do the same, promoting independence instead of dependence on others.

Friendship offers valuable support, and therapy can be beneficial as well. It's crucial to have someone with whom you can discuss your feelings. Nevertheless, it becomes problematic if you feel unable to cope without a therapist or professional support. Many practitioners and organizations are designed to promote ongoing appointments. Although they intend to assist you in making progress, their financial stability also depends on your continued visits.

Typically, the emphasis isn't on enabling your healing so thoroughly that future sessions become unnecessary. Instead, it prompts you to share enough to motivate a return for deeper discussions. Speaking Freedom, Love Gang, and Good Head Group aim to empower you towards self-sufficiency, assisting you in processing your emotions and thoughts independently before applying the insights gained from these experiences.

Please avoid using your healing to evaluate or belittle others for not being as advanced as you; rather, assist them in feeling complete. Motivate those around you by recounting your journey of overcoming obstacles and fostering their growth. Interact with individuals at their current state.

The emphasis isn't on finding individuals who need help. It's about uplifting everyone we encounter. It could be as straightforward as sharing a smile. Remember, it goes beyond just feelings. Whether it's greeting someone, engaging in conversation, or recognizing that someone might benefit from a theory you know, share it with them. Explain how it has helped you and might be helpful for them, too.

The Great Commission encourages you to recognize your purpose and love, prompting you to intentionally choose to be a role model for others by embodying love and compassion. Strive to be a living representation of self-love, discipline, determination, focus, and positive energy. You have the power to manifest everything you desire for yourself. Once you've secured this for yourself, remember the airplane advice: put on your oxygen mask first.

After securing your oxygen mask, you can assist those around you. Similarly, after establishing your purpose, confidence, and knowledge that facilitate growth, you can support others in their development with what you've learned. These are not merely concepts you heard fail for someone else; they are insights you've implemented in your life that have truly made an impact.

Sharing yourself with the world, whether on a large or small scale, can sometimes feel overwhelming. However, the goal is to express yourself and be who you are. Avoid molding your personality to fit others' expectations or doing what you think they want you to do. It's essential to learn to trust yourself, have faith in God within you, and believe in the vision, goals, and path God guides you on. Next, we'll discuss various gifts, talents, and skills. When I refer to 'gifts,' I don't mean Christmas presents.

I refer to your innate abilities as a natural talent or skill that others cannot perform without training or guidance. A gift, whether a physical present or an inherent ability, only becomes a true gift when it is shared with someone else without expectation of payment. Typically, being described as gifted and talented indicates a person who excels in intellectual pursuits, creativity, the arts, or leadership, or has expertise in a specific academic domain and needs support to cultivate that gift effectively.

Gifts are frequently mentioned in religious contexts as signs of the spirit of God residing within an individual. It's important to distinguish between a talent and the monetary talent referenced in Roman times. A talent is a unique ability that enables someone to excel in a particular area. Talent is innate, akin to giftedness.

Talent is typically a natural ability that can benefit from nurturing or development, similar to being naturally gifted. Singing and dancing are typical examples of talent. On the other hand, giftedness is more about extraordinary intelligence and cognitive abilities. A skill, in contrast, requires deliberate effort; it is knowledge gained through learning and practice. Therefore, talent can be viewed as the depth and breadth of a skill, with a skill potentially evolving into a talent and giftedness.

Ironically, talent is now a means of earning money when, at one time, it functioned as a form of currency. This shift reflects a shift where abilities are exchanged for money, contrasting with when money was simply available without needing to leverage one's skills.

Let's define ability as the skills or means to accomplish a task. Various abilities include multitasking, which allows one to perform multiple activities simultaneously, depending on the assignment or objective. So now let me explain how skills, talents, gifts, and abilities in general relate to spiritual human behavior.

2013 I stated, "I believe God has given us a skill and a gift. The skill is what we do naturally with little effort for fun." Skills include writing, designing, singing, fashion, or even waiting tables. I define a skill as a polished ability. Conversely, a gift signifies a distinctive talent that can profoundly influence lives. Depending on the person, this gift can manifest positively and negatively. Your skill acts as a means to your calling, while your gift represents that calling, enhancing your abilities.

God never does things the way we expect. We want to reach a specific destination, but we want to do it our way, even though the path God reveals will still lead to what we desire. It's like receiving only half of a vision. There is a purpose behind everything. Often, we commit to things without realizing that they might be for a specific season, for the birth of a child, or for creating a job that helps someone reach their true potential. Thus, it's not about whether there is a job title for it; when something is meant for you, one will be created. Just because your purpose involves something that doesn't exist doesn't mean you cannot bring it to life.

Even though you wanted things to go one way, God created a way for you to get you where you want to be and where you need to be. If it unfolds differently than anticipated, will you let that cause you to overlook God's guidance? It's more about pursuing what will lead you to your promised destination rather than seeking immediate satisfaction. You cannot claim to trust God if you struggle to accept His direction when it doesn't align with your expectations.

Many people find prayer challenging. They may request guidance but struggle to embrace the responses they receive. It can feel safer to conform rather than stand out. Those with unique gifts or talents are often more susceptible to substance abuse, stemming from a sense of not belonging. They might doubt their ability to achieve the purpose God intended for them or feel trapped by societal norms, prompting them to shy away from their true calling and abilities. This constant guidance on what not to do can lead them to question their sanity.

This is relevant for children with ADHD and other conditions that affect brain function, particularly those with high levels of intellect or different cognitive styles. Often, there aren't sufficient stimulating activities for these children, leading their unique brilliance to manifest as disruptive behavior. My talent is helping individuals navigate their lives effectively. My gift is prophetic. What is your talent and gift?

When delving into spiritual human behavior, it's essential to recognize and embrace your distinct qualities, as they may relate to your calling, talents, and gifts. Everyone has unique abilities, but these can vary greatly, and we should refrain from limiting individuals to a narrow view of their potential. Pay attention to what comes to you effortlessly and intuitively—those activities that flow naturally. This is often your gift.

Often, your gift is something you engage in without even realizing it. Others seek your advice because you offer it easily and provide reliable guidance consistently. This ability could very well be your gift. You perform it so instinctively that you might not see it as a gift, but those around you notice, appreciate, and acknowledge this talent in you.

You need to understand, acknowledge, and utilize your gift for yourself instead of continually giving it away to others. Now is the moment to start using that gift to heal and empower yourself, ultimately making yourself complete. Once you attain this sense of wholeness, you'll be better equipped to assist others in addressing their brokenness and finding their paths to completeness.

Most of the gifts mentioned here are rooted in a biblical perspective, providing insight into the foundational principles upon which this nation was established.

The first gift is *administration*, which involves guiding the community towards fulfilling God-given objectives and directives through effective planning, organization, and oversight of others in pursuit of the current mission, purpose, or vision.

The gift of an *apostle* is to be sent forth to new frontiers with the gospel, offering assistance, providing leadership to church bodies and fellowships, and upholding authority in spiritual matters related to the church community.

The gift of *celibacy* involves choosing to stay single willingly, without remorse, while managing sexual urges to serve God without distraction.

The gift of *discernment* distinguishes truth from error, assessing whether behavior or teachings come from God, human ego, mistakes, or external influences. It empowers you to intuitively sense when someone is lying versus when they are being truthful.

Much like an Earth Angel, the gift of *evangelism* serves as a messenger of good news for those in need.

The gift of *exhortation* involves supporting someone with uplifting words of encouragement, comfort, consolation, and guidance to help them achieve their full potential as God intended.

The gift of *faith* involves being firmly convinced of God's power and promises to fulfill His will and purpose. It allows one to exhibit such confidence in Him and His word that circumstances and obstacles do not undermine the conviction and determination to reach the goal.

The gift of *giving* involves freely and happily sharing your material resources without any expectation of receiving something back. Essentially, it means giving selflessly and not anticipating anything in return from others, but trusting in God.

The gift of *healing* is a means by which God makes people whole, physically, emotionally, mentally, or spiritually.

The gift of *help* is to provide support or assistance to others in the body, allowing them to focus on ministry.

The gift of *hospitality* involves warmly welcoming familiar faces and strangers into your home or church to serve those needing food or lodging. However, it is essential to prioritize safety and exercise caution regarding who you invite into your space.

The gift of *knowledge* involves striving to learn extensively about matters connected to your purpose by gathering and analyzing ample information, alongside the wisdom received from God.

The gift of *leadership* is to stand before the people and attend to the direction of the body with such care and diligence that it inspires them to pursue collective goals, dreams, and visions.

The gift of *mercy* is to be sensitive to those who are suffering, to feel genuine sympathy for their misery, to speak words of compassion, and, more importantly, to care for them through loving deeds that help alleviate their distress.

The gift of *miracles* enables God to perform mighty deeds, which witnesses acknowledge as supernatural in origin and significance.

The gift of a *missionary* is the ability to serve within another culture.

The gift of *prophecy* is to proclaim God's message to His people.

The gift of *service* involves identifying unnecessary tasks in God's work, no matter how menial, and utilizing available resources to complete the job.

The gift of *teaching* is instructing others toward their purpose by conveying essential information logically and non-systematically, fostering accurate understanding and personal growth.

The gift of *tongues* enables one to speak in a language not previously learned, allowing unbelievers to hear God's message in their language and the body to be edified.

The gift of *voluntary poverty* involves consciously choosing to live an impoverished lifestyle to serve and assist others with your material resources.

The gift of *wisdom* is the ability to apply knowledge to life, making spiritual truths relevant and practical for decision-making and everyday situations. These are a few examples of such gifts.

If you're taking classes with Goodhead Group, you will be assigned to take a test to determine your spiritual gift. Most of these tests are designed to give you a list of questions and responses. They will tell you what's likely to be your highest level of giftedness and what is your lowest.

Imagine you're skilled at organizing your top point system for the gifted test, perhaps in administration. Conversely, someone inclined towards outreach might excel in evangelism.

Tests and methods are available to assess your giftedness, identify areas of focus, and determine what subjects to study to enhance your effectiveness in your gift. It's important to understand that natural talents often serve as the medium through which your spiritual gifts are expressed. For instance, a vocalist might showcase the spiritual gift of evangelism through their musical abilities.

Another list of gifts lists words of wisdom, words of knowledge, faith, the gift of healing, the gift of prophecy, miracles, various tongues and their interpretation, discernment, intercession (which is prayer), and dream interpretation.

Words of wisdom are based on what you've learned and experienced, and they help others learn from the experiences you've overcome with your words. The next set of gifts I will list are often considered to be psychic abilities or a sixth sense.

These are not superhuman abilities from fiction or anything like that. These are real people in the real world, experiencing their perception and human abilities that are more developed than everyone else's. Teleportation is the ability to undergo materialization and disappearance, or teleportation of an object.

Astral projection, or mental projection, refers to the capacity to send out the astral body's consciousness consciously. This phenomenon is linked to the experience of the astral body feeling temporarily detached from the physical form, similar to an out-of-body experience.

Aura reading involves perceiving the energy fields surrounding individuals, locations, or objects.

Automatic writing is creating drawings or text without deliberate intention, yet it carries significant meaning.

Clairaudience is the ability to acquire information by paranormal auditory means. That means you hear things nobody else hears, and they're accurate.

Claircognizance is the ability to acquire psychic knowledge through intrinsic knowledge.

Clairgustance is the ability to taste without physical contact. Have you ever smelled something and wondered why? You don't have it in your mouth, but you can taste it. That's what that is.

Clairofaction is the ability to access spiritual or mediumistic knowledge through smell.

Clairvoyance is the ability to perceive people, objects, locations, or physical events via extrasensory perception.

Divination is the ability to gain insight into a situation using abnormal means.

Dowsing is the ability to locate water, sometimes using a dowsing rod.

Energy manipulation, or energy work, is manipulating physical or non-physical energy with one's mind.

Energy medicine is healing with one's own empathetic or mental, spiritual energy.

Levitation is the ability to float or fly by mystical means.

Mediumship, or channeling, is the ability to speak with spirits.

Precognition or premonition is the ability to perceive future events.

Prophecy is the ability to predict the future.

Psychic surgery involves removing a disease or disorder within or over the body tissue via energetic incision that heals immediately afterwards. Telekinesis, or psychokinesis, is the ability to manipulate objects with one's mind.

Remote viewing is seeing distant or unseen targets using extrasensory perception.

Retrocognition is the ability to perceive past events supernaturally.

Second sight is the ability to see the future and past events or to perceive information not present to the physical senses in the form of vision. It's also called remote viewing or being a seer.

Telepathy is the ability to transmit or receive thoughts supernaturally. The gift of empathy is the ability to compassionately identify with someone else's difficulties or challenging times so that they can be sustained.

Although some of these abilities may be controversial, it is best to help you identify with natural abilities if you understand both sides of the spiritual world. The psychic world is not contradictory to the spiritual gifts in the Bible. They are very similar and should be used to balance and understand each other.

When it comes to gifts, talents, skills, and abilities, particularly gifts, it's crucial to find balance. Avoid letting energy vampires—those who drain your positive energy—overwhelm you. These individuals often arrive with a negative aura that can leave you feeling depleted, as they take from you without giving anything in return.

Protecting yourself and recognizing your identity is crucial to shielding yourself against those who might want to manipulate you because of your gifts. Some individuals will gravitate towards you because of your abilities and talents, while others may seek your guidance to enhance their giftedness and skills.

Some individuals will be called to assist you in nurturing your talents, gifts, and skills. Others will collaborate with you to empower yourselves and others, fostering a sense of community and growth akin to a soul family. However, there will also be those who merely wish to take advantage of your gifts.

As a gifted, healed, or whole individual in this role, part of your responsibility is to ensure your protection while assisting others. Helping others effectively requires that you first prioritize your healing and self-care. Additionally, you must learn how to shield yourself from those who resist healing and seek to drain your energy for their selfish ends.

Some individuals find comfort in their brokenness, as it draws the attention they think they desire. However, they fail to understand that true healing comes from recognizing their gifts, comprehending their skills, and maximizing their talents and abilities. This journey allows them to obtain the attention they crave without feeling broken, playing the victim, or diminishing their self-worth so that others will notice them. Both lists aim to help create a sense of balance.

For deep Christian believers, spiritual gifts associated with psychic abilities are included in the discussion. If you are not a Christian but wish to learn about spiritual gifts, you can refer to the list of psychic abilities.

Both lists complement each other, no matter how different they seem. A few things were not previously listed, like intercession and prayer. The gift of prayer is a gift where some people are gifted at praying for others, getting results, manifesting, and helping people overcome through prayer, which is their natural gift.

Some people are great and gifted at interpreting dreams. This means that you can tell them about a dream that you've had, and if you don't understand it, they can help you better understand your dream as you describe it to them. The gift of interpretation is like the interpreter of dreams; it's interpreting diverse tongues when someone speaks in tongues.

Understanding your unique gifts, skills, talents, and abilities is the goal of ensuring that each individual contributes effectively. If everyone stops trying to imitate one another and instead focuses on their unique abilities, they can excel in being themselves. When individuals are great at embracing their authentic selves and pursuing their purpose, far more can be accomplished than when everyone attempts to conform to others.

We are all designed to be different, created for unique purposes, means, and abilities. We are meant to collaborate in various groups globally, supporting one another to improve our world. However, if we constantly compete, strive to emulate others, and try to conform to the roles defined for us, we will never realize our full potential.

The essence is this: if every joint supply represents discovering your purpose, then connecting with that purpose allows you to be a gift. Being a vessel for God is the ultimate gift of all.

That is the greatest blessing, the most remarkable grace we can receive. If everyone spoke up about their challenges, we would address every issue. If everyone became the support they needed as children, many more problems would be resolved, as we would be bridging the gaps that were left empty for us.

Become the person you needed as a child, embody who you aspire to be for others, and provide the guidance they seek. If you lack knowledge, seek information to enhance your awareness. In this information age, you can learn anything you desire. With just a quick Internet search, you can gain valuable insights.

Are you ready to become a certified plumber online? You have the potential, but we also want to ensure you gain practical experience. The most important aspect of spiritual human behavior isn't just developing theories; it's applying those theories in real life and allowing others to utilize them for monitoring the outcomes during what we refer to as the beta testing period.

During the beta test, you harness your gifts, talents, skills, knowledge, and additional theories to evolve into your best self. We have enabled numerous individuals to implement this knowledge, demonstrating its effectiveness. What you believe the world lacks is precisely what you should embody.

If you notice its absence, you either require it or must embody it. Use your talents and abilities for positive purposes rather than for wrongdoing or manipulation. You have the option to employ each gift for either good or evil. However, regardless of your choice, karma will be inescapable. What goes around comes around, and this principle remains true. You can create positive karma through good deeds and by helping others constructively, or you can use your gift for deceit. Yet, your ability will continue to exist regardless of whether you are misusing it.

The karma you cultivate internally and the tangible outcomes you create will speak volumes. Therefore, using your abilities wisely ensures you foster positive karma for your future. Understanding your skills, gifts, and talents is essential to fulfilling your purpose, as all these elements work together to achieve the mission, vision, and the life that God has created for you to complete.

When you possess a gift intended for God's purpose yet choose not to assist others, you inadvertently harm them by withholding the very blessing God entrusted to you. Recognizing and utilizing your spiritual gifts to support those in need is crucial. Deja vu, dreams, premonitions, spiritual gifts, or natural abilities should be employed to aid God's people.

If you resonate with any of these spiritual gifts or psychic abilities, I encourage you to conduct research. This will help you gain a deeper understanding of yourself and the gift. If I had to choose which gift I most relate to, it would be the gift of foresight, as I can sometimes perceive events before they are likely to occur.

Some aspects rely on the specific circumstances and influencing factors. The rest comes more naturally; I can just feel it. I also connect with automatic writing, where I begin by asking a question or writing down my ideas. Before I realize it, a simple thought can evolve into a more complex, detailed thought process or body of knowledge. While writing or typing, I'm frequently unsure of the source of the information. It feels as if what I'm expressing originates from deep inside me. Occasionally, I need to reread my words to grasp their meaning and implications for the future.

Sometimes, I can intuitively grasp other people's thoughts and conversations, sensing their emotions without magic or trickery. Occasionally, I find myself flooded with a strong feeling, emotion, or connection to something. Additionally, I experience dreams and waking visions, where I can vividly dream, which unfold in my mind like a film or television program.

That's how clear the image is for me. There are also moments when those dreams manifest, I encounter things in reality that I dreamed about, or an extension of the dream occurs in real life. Occasionally, I can envision the outcome.

I can recognize someone's potential when they embrace their highest calling and acknowledge their unique qualities. Typically, I assist people in discovering the best path for themselves. Additionally, I support others in their healing process through different types of information, some guided by spirituality and others grounded in knowledge. My psychology studies have enhanced my psychic abilities and heightened my sensitivity to extrasensory perceptions.

I have realized that I am a strong manifestor. I often articulate my thoughts, which frequently come to fruition. My spiritual essence often connects with the departed or those who have passed on.

Sometimes, God provides an experience similar to mediumship, allowing me to serve as a vessel for healing those dealing with loss. For several years, I have dedicated myself to studying and deepening my understanding of my gifts and abilities. This personal journey empowers me to assist others in recognizing their talents and skills. Many aspects of natural gifts and abilities are inherent to all individuals.

Our sense of smell parallels our ability to foresee or trust our intuition. The key distinction is that society has taught us to recognize our five senses: touch, hearing, sight, smell, and taste. Although often overlooked, communication forms a significant part of our sensory experience. All of these factors contribute to our identity as humans. As human beings, we possess senses that we are not accustomed to using or understanding, as they do not fit within the broader conceptual framework established for our lives.

Some of these concepts remain untaught or unillustrated due to their inability to be confirmed by "scientific fact." Nonetheless, much scientific knowledge stems from trial and error, highlighting the importance of experiencing certain things for learning.

To grasp any natural or spiritual gifts, or any psychic type of gifts where you're actually in tune with all your senses, consider this: when I feel the hairs on my arm rise while conversing with someone, it signifies that God's spirit is at work.

This is my cue to convey to that individual that what I'm sharing is crucial, as it provokes a reaction beyond the typical five learned senses. It's somewhat like a gut feeling, but it differs slightly. While not all these abilities are necessarily special, some individuals may be capable of running at super-fast speeds, whereas others cannot.

Every gift, talent, and ability is distinctive to you. While not everyone excels in art or possesses drawing skills, some excel as artists in various fields. You may have a talent for singing, but playing an instrument may not be your forte.

Some individuals effortlessly possess these natural talents, while others need training to perceive, understand, and experience them. Therefore, it's crucial for each of us to invest time in understanding our unique qualities.

Indeed, we are all human. We possess blood and originate from a mother and a father. Each of us has senses; although not everyone consistently uses common sense, everyone has physical senses. For the most part, all individuals experience attraction. All can experience arousal. Anyone can feel anger. Anyone can sense fear.

When people become attuned to God's spirit, they can experience happiness, joy, and the fullness of God's spirit flowing through their lives.

The spirit of God awakens your soul and purpose, helping you comprehend your journey on earth. Your gifts, skills, and talents are meant to guide you towards fulfilling the promise and destiny set for you before your arrival. Often, when we start to hold back and suppress our gifts—not just our thoughts—but also our skills and abilities, or when we lack opportunities for their growth, we risk diminishing our true selves.

It's essential to recognize that not all these gifts are connected to athletic skills. Similarly, not all of them pertain to musical talents. Some abilities may face stigma or shame. While some people have vivid dreams, others might have perceptions beyond the commonplace. Additionally, some individuals can see auras, and others can communicate with the deceased.

All of these are gifts, no matter your perspective. Though you might view a psychic as malevolent, they are no more evil than a prophet in a church. They each utilize their gifts to assist.

This concept applies universally to everyone in the world.

How are you using your spiritual gifts, natural gifts, talents, and abilities to help improve the lives of those around you and the world? You create a whole new world by influencing and setting a positive example for others as you grow. It's a trickle effect, impacting not just your immediate surroundings but the entire globe.

The better you understand yourself, the less judgmental you become towards others. As you recognize and value your gifts, you will also appreciate the unique talents and abilities of those around you. Ultimately, spiritual human behavior aims to attain self-acceptance, enabling us to encourage others to accept and embrace their journeys. This mutual understanding stems from our self-acceptance and comprehension of our paths.

Recognizing that each person has a distinct journey shaped by their backgrounds and experiences reveals how these factors influence our identities. If we view life as a school aimed at uncovering our true selves, rather than simply fitting into societal norms, we can enhance our self-awareness. The greater our understanding of our individuality, the more we can appreciate our unique gifts, fostering stronger connections with others.

When we each pursue our unique paths—me with my work and yours—we all tap into our strengths, no matter how alike or different they might be. Regardless of what we excel in, whether singing, writing, running, speaking, or thinking, focusing on cultivating our strengths while working on our weaknesses allows us to feel truly gifted. Everyone possesses their special talents, intended to fulfill their unique purpose in life.

Now Do Your Part in Spreading Love in the World.

Section 7, The Love Warranty.

This section will explore how love brings everything together, whether self-love or love within the community. We will discuss how embracing love fosters personal growth and impacts your surroundings, spirit, and those you interact with. Before we begin, I would like to share a chapter from a book that might resonate with you. Throughout this section, I will revisit parts of this chapter to help you understand its significance by the conclusion, as it will mark the end of the book.

As you embark on your healing journey, you naturally attract individuals who have healed and align with the direction of your purpose. The majority of your soul family is included in your soul contract. Thus, once you enter the world through your mother's womb, a specific destination has already been set for you.

Your perspective determines the specific place you find yourself in. Consider a person you encounter at a certain point in their life; even if you alter some of their decisions, their mindset may remain constant, and the circumstances may not change significantly, yet their environment and situation could differ considerably. This chapter aims to provide clarity and perspective on these dynamics.

When discussing soul family, it may encompass your spouse, friends, partnerships, and everything else typically included. If you're married and have been married before, your aspiration for a meaningful and purposeful life may challenge your marriage as you strive to become the best version of yourself. The essential aspect of sustaining a marriage lies in both partners actively engaging in personal growth, maturation, and alignment, each as willing participants in the evolution of the relationship.

When one partner chooses to grow while the other prefers to stay the same, it can create issues. Your elevation may stall if the other person is reluctant to develop and isn't on the same level as you. A critical point about promoting freedom is that we can assist in healing and restoring many genuinely happy marriages that are meant to endure. On the other hand, those who are unhappily stuck yet pretend to be content may face divorce and separation as they become more aligned with their purposes.

If a spouse or significant other refuses to participate or is unable to. In that case, you can work to find ways to share information about your progress and growth passively. However, remember that you cannot compel someone to grow if they are content with their current situation. While this book isn't about religion, I encourage you to read 1 Corinthians chapter 13. It's a chapter discussing love, and I'll break it down to help you see how it relates to your life.

If I speak in the tongues of men or angels but do not have love, I am only a resounding gong or a clanging cymbal. If I have the gift of prophecy and can fathom all mysteries and all knowledge, and if I have a faith that can move mountains, but do not have love, I am nothing. If I give all I possess to people experiencing poverty and give over my body to hardship that I may boast, but do not have love, I gain nothing.

Love is patient.

Love is kind. It does not envy.

Love does not boast. Love is not proud. Love does not dishonor others.

Love is not self-seeking. Love is not easily angered. Love keeps no record of wrongs and easily forgives.

Love does not delight in evil, but rejoices in truth. It always protects. Love always trusts.

Love always hopes. Love always perseveres. Love never fails.

But where there are prophecies, they may cease to exist. Where there are tongues, they may be stilled and quiet. Where there is knowledge, that knowledge will pass away and have no relevance.

We know only in part, and we prophesy only based on the part we are exposed to. But when completeness comes, what was in part at one point will disappear.

When I was a child, I talked like a child.

I thought and reasoned like a child. When I became a man or a woman—better know who's reading—I put my childhood behind me.

For now, we only see a reflection as in a mirror. Then we shall see face to face. Now I know in part. Then I shall know fully, even as I am fully known.

Now these three remain: faith, hope, and love. But the greatest of these is love.

This is significant because I read it in the New International Version of the Bible when examining it. I will also refer to the Message Bible for additional clarity. I'm focusing on this particular chapter because it offers a guideline for understanding what love truly is. I want to add a few aspects of love not covered in this chapter.

I want to explain the childlike nature that's missing in this chapter.

Listen, love is not weak.

Love is not timid.

Love is not intimidated and is not intimidating.

Love is full of life.

It is both joy and a challenge. It is finding strengths and identifying weaknesses.

Love is discipline and freedom.

Love is not passive. Loving someone doesn't mean you should let them mistreat or exploit you. To truly love others, you must also be self-aware, value yourself, and care for those around you.

When you appreciate and love yourself, you eliminate the barriers that lead to judgment of others.

The Message Bible says,

If I speak with human eloquence and angelic ecstasy but don't love, I am nothing but a creaking of a rusty gate. If I speak God's word with power, I reveal all of his mysteries and make everything as plain as day.

And if I have faith that says to a mountain move, jump, and it jumps, but I do not love, I am nothing. If I give everything I own to people experiencing poverty and even go to the stake to be burned as a martyr, but I don't love, I've got nowhere. So no matter what I say, what I believe, and what I do, I am bankrupt without love.

Love never gives up. Love cares more for others than for self. Love doesn't want what it doesn't have.

Love doesn't strut. Love doesn't have a swelled head. Love doesn't force itself on others.

Love isn't always me first. Love doesn't fly off the handle. Love doesn't keep score of others' sins.

Love doesn't reveal when others grovel. Love isn't happy when others are groveling.

Love takes pleasure in the flowering of truth.

Love puts up with anything. Love trusts God always. Love always looks for the best.

Love never looks back, but love keeps going to the end. Love never dies. Inspired speech will be over someday.

Praying in tongues will end. Understanding will reach its limits. We know only a portion of the truth, and what we say about God is always incomplete.

But when the complete arrives, the incomplete will be canceled. When I was an infant at my mother's breast, I cooed like an infant. When I grew up, I left those infant ways for good.

We don't yet see things clearly. We're squinting in a fog, peering through a mist, but it won't be long before the weather clears up and the sun shines bright. We'll see it all then.

See it as clear as God sees us, knowing him directly as he knows us. But for right now, until that completeness, we have three things to lead us towards that consummation. Trust steadily in God. Hope unswervingly. Love extravagantly. And the best of the three is love.

The question is, what is love, and how is love the warranty? When love is used, whether the situation is good or bad, it always gets you the best results because love is balanced within. Love is a feeling or a strong, constant affection for a person. It is an attraction that can also include sexual desire, not to be confused with lust.

When discussing relationships, love involves giving in every sense, including a physical connection through sex. However, the key distinction between love and lust lies in the willingness to sacrifice and prioritize another person's needs over your own. This implies that it is not always about putting yourself first. Instead, the love for them means being committed to giving them the advantage.

If someone loves you, they will give you the advantage and meet you halfway, potentially compromising or agreeing to disagree. The goal is to find balance and common ground that fosters love's growth. This applies particularly to relationships.

It is essential to differentiate between lust and love, as we often meet people and become attracted to their surface qualities. This can lead us to mistake our feelings for love when we are merely drawn to their outward appearance, focusing on superficial aspects.

At times, we can deeply understand and love someone. However, there are two types of love: "I love you," where we are purposeful for each other, meant to be together to build a life, have children, and stay connected forever. The second is also "I love you." Still, in this sense, we are meant to support each other by utilizing our gifts to complement one another, build businesses, friendships, or create something that doesn't involve romantic or sexual relationships.

Often, we meet people we like and feel lust for them. We mistakenly assume it's love because of the mutual attraction, only to discover later that it was lust, which doesn't last when the relationship isn't meant to be.

For a relationship to thrive over the long term, we must genuinely complement one another. It's important to differentiate between love and lust, as you may feel lustful toward someone who is truly meant to be a lifelong friend. Such confusion can threaten friendships that might otherwise foster successful business ventures or future family support.

Recognizing what you don't want in a relationship is essential for defining what you want and understanding what aligns with your identity and life goals. Love genuinely acts as the catalyst for your aspirations. Positive karma and everything your soul desires arise from a base of authentic love. If you aim to manifest your dreams but hold onto negativity, mistreat others, or lack a loving attitude, these feelings can hinder fulfilling your deepest desires.

If you're feeling down or depressed, whatever you create could reflect that negativity. Consequently, anything you manifest during such a time might not align with your true intentions or endure, as your mindset and heart are not aligned. However, by cleansing your heart, practicing forgiveness, and embracing self-acceptance and self-love, you enable yourself to offer others forgiveness, love, and acceptance.

Accepting others for who they are doesn't always mean keeping them in your life. Sometimes, truly accepting and loving people means distancing yourself, as self-love is important too. If someone, a place, or an experience doesn't enhance your self-love, it detracts from it.

If someone isn't beneficial for your goals and future, you must prioritize self-love by recognizing when a relationship, partnership, or visit should be ended. It's not worth jeopardizing your emotional well-being or essence for someone who doesn't belong in your life. I often share this advice with my friends or acquaintances. If I'm not helping you grow or fostering your positive mindset, please feel free to distance yourself from me. I wouldn't want to contribute to stagnation in your life or surroundings.

Love serves as the action code because when we love ourselves, it influences our perspective. This love can either lead us to have a positive or negative outlook. When you accept and love yourself, you will have a more positive attitude toward life and your surroundings since you better understand your direction, identity, and purpose.

Ultimately, love will unlock your greatest purpose by eliminating childish behaviors. This doesn't mean losing your innocence or capability for childlike faith, but rather letting go of pettiness, mood swings, selfishness for attention, and a sense of being spoiled.

You must begin to love and accept yourself. As your self-love increases, so will your ability to love and positively engage with others. Transforming these aspects enables you to manifest your dreams differently.

Living in love involves a lifestyle focused on uplifting others, assisting when possible, refraining from judgment, displaying compassion and sympathy, and seeking peace. However, love can manifest as directness, honesty, correction, and the readiness to apologize when necessary. Understanding that walking in love does not mean allowing others to mistreat you is essential.

If someone is harmful and unworthy of your life, kindly remove them from it. Remember, you are the CEO of your own life.

You are the chief executive officer in your life. Not even God can do anything unless you allow him to do it. You determine who and what stays in your life.

Your healing deepens as you grow in love, leading to a greater understanding of compassion, sympathy, and peace. Authentic fulfillment is the accurate measure of success, rooted in inner tranquility and living a life that brings you joy.

7 Types of Love:

Eros is a sexual or passionate love based on modern-day romance, thought to have been sparked by Cupid's arrow.

Philia is a shared goodwill based on friendship. Aristotle believed people bear goodwill for one of three reasons. The person is helpful, good, or a reasonably good person. A virtue and very rational

Storge is love amongst family or developed in familiar areas and is a natural type of affection.

Agape is a universal love that's without condition for all that strangers and nature give a helper. It's high because it's based on compassion for others you aren't familiar with. Agape is just being nice and loving to people, places, and things, no matter how familiar you are with them, simply because they deserve love.

Ludus is a playful, uncommitted love, such as flirting, and it encompasses the art of seduction focused on fun.

Pragma is conditional love based on reason, duty, or a sense of obligation. It is most common in arranged marriages and political pairings.

Philautia is self-love, whether healthy or unhealthy, based on personal and spiritual beliefs.

Self-love is the basis for loving and expressing love toward others. Unhealthy self-love is thinking you're above everybody, displaying haughty behavior, and putting others down. Healthy self-love is knowing that everybody deserves love.

Everybody is human and equal. Self-love is about self-esteem. How well you live, love, and esteem yourself will set the tone for how well you can love and esteem others.

Soul Connections

The greater and deeper your self-love, the more love you can share with others. But what exactly is a soul family, and what does soul love mean? A *soul family* serves as the spiritual counterpart to your biological family, although they differ significantly. As you nurture self-love and grow internally, you will draw in those who resonate with you.

People may come from various backgrounds and have unique circumstances that help them connect with you. However, as you start to love yourself and accept, embrace, and express your true self, distinct from who you've felt pressured to be by societal expectations or definitions of success, you will naturally attract what resonates with you. It's essential to recognize that what you attract and what you engage with are not the same. This ties back to the hold-up theory and the paradox: while you may draw in something that seems destined to be part of your life forever, it might be there for just a season or a specific reason.

Sometimes, we confuse those meant to be in our lives for the long term with people only there temporarily. They may come into our lives to help us reach a specific place, lesson, or development. Additionally, they may attract us to help clear past karmic energies, whether that karma originates from us or previous generations that we need to work through now. While discussing soul families, I would also like to address soulmates and twin flames.

A *soulmate* is meant to connect with you at a specific moment to assist you in learning lessons, navigating experiences, or achieving a more profound sense of completeness within yourself. Soulmates aren't limited to romantic connections; they can also be found in friends, companions, or pets.

Friendship can also lead you to a soulmate, as soul families connect with you on a deep, soulful level. These are your soulmates, who unite for a common mission or purpose, or to enjoy life alongside you. The key distinction between a soulmate and a twin flame is that a twin flame acts as a mirror to your soul, reflecting all aspects of who you are and aiding in your self-discovery.

A *soul friend* represents the most prevalent form of relational connection. You've selected these individuals because your ego, intellect, or emotions resonate harmoniously with theirs. You align in tastes, interests, beliefs, humor, and values.

Although this bond may not be as profound as that of a soul companion, the presence of a soul friend is often harmonious. Occasionally, friends also act as soul teachers, but we select our soul family influenced by inner factors.

A *soul teacher* is an individual who enters your life to impart a lesson or assist you in gaining a clearer understanding of certain aspects of life.

A soul teacher does not have to be someone who teaches purposefully; instead, their presence in your life leads you to learn valuable lessons. These teachers can take many forms, such as family members, friends, former partners, wanderers, and even adversaries, all of whom can impart important lessons. You draw them into your life because there are lessons you are meant to learn from them.

Companionship closely resembles soul friendship and is occasionally called a soul mate. In addition to romantic attraction, soul companions can be either males or females, including friends and family members. While soul friends resonate with our ego identities, soul companions share a more profound soulful harmony.

In Greek mythology, while a twin soul is seen as our other half, it's believed that originally our souls were unified, and the gods split them into two. When we locate that other half, we become whole again, akin to the portrayal of love in the chapter I read. This chapter discusses how, in finding wholeness, you begin to see yourself instead of just a reflection. This idea resonates with the concept of a soul family; if the teachings of Corinthians represent your understanding of love—how to acquire and sustain it—then recognizing yourself in another soul signifies a profound connection beyond the ordinary.

While this connection may not last forever, if it is your twin flame, it will ignite aspects of yourself that you might not have previously recognized. Anyone who comes into your life serves one of three purposes: a season, a reason, or a lifetime. When someone enters for a reason, it may be tied to karmic resolution, lessons for personal growth, or elements of your past that you need to address to evolve.

When someone comes into your life for a season, they are brought into your journey for a specific time to help you navigate challenges you may face. In contrast, lifelong companions and members of your soul family tend to be around much longer. You grow, build, and evolve together, forming a supportive community for raising your children and fully embracing life.

These lifetime individuals will be purposeful, complementary figures in your life, who possess valuable qualities to share and seek what you offer. It's important to understand that a twin flame can share many similarities with a soulmate and can also be your soulmate, but to a more intense degree.

Karmic relationships and partnerships may share characteristics with twin flames, as they often evoke your emotional wounds and can be intense. However, they do not stem from the same soul. Your paths do not truly align, nor do you participate in a sacred union with these relationships.

A twin flame and your soul family aim to help you become the best versions of yourselves in pursuit of wholeness and a deeper understanding of love. By embodying the true essence of love, you will connect with others who share your beliefs about love.

This section isn't about relationships, but it's essential to touch on specific relationships, particularly those connected to the soul, as they are central to this book.

Love and Forgiveness

As you learn to understand and accept yourself, you also start to embrace others for who they are, even if they haven't reached their full potential or differ.

Love shows compassion for those who are unique. It recognizes our differences and acknowledges our distinct backgrounds and upbringings.

Everyone comes from different parental backgrounds, shaping our unique identities. While life can feel like a collaborative effort, it truly becomes so only when we connect with our soul family. Without that connection, we may aimlessly pursue goals we were never meant to achieve. So, what makes love the ultimate guarantee? Love binds everything together.

Love allows you to believe more, grow more, and have confidence in what you know you deserve because of what you are willing to put up with and put out. You deserve what you're willing to give, and when you're willing to love, you are also allowing yourself to be willing to receive love. Love, like spiritual human behavior, is about healing and growing.

By applying the theories in this book for healing, you'll start to embrace all the experiences you've lived through as essential to your journey. You'll gradually escape chaos, drama, and disruptions interfering with your peace or diverting you from your purpose. However, before this can happen, you must clarify your purpose, recognize what you love about yourself, understand your identity, and envision who you wish to become.

What does your best self look like? Where do you envision yourself at your highest potential? What is your escape version, and how can you love yourself enough to reveal it? A crucial aspect of self-love involves removing your filters. Discard all that you've adopted to gain acceptance from others or even from yourself.

You should stand before a mirror and see the person God has made you. Acknowledge God's image in you, showcasing His likeness. This indicates that your authentic self is in harmony with your intended path. When we start altering ourselves—internally and externally—or adapting to others' expectations, we compromise our genuine selves. These changes result in bitterness, unhappiness, and a sense of emptiness.

To achieve fulfillment, it's essential to prioritize what is best for you and understand your purpose. You must understand your preferences and aversions. Embrace the authentic, unfiltered version of yourself, especially if no one else does. Self-love is your guarantee; even if others do not accept you, loving yourself ensures you will achieve whatever you want.

Your ambitious determination drives you forward. It's your love for yourself and appreciation of who you are, independent of weaves, lashes, makeup, clothing, shoes, homes, cars, or other superficial adornments.

Do you truly love yourself? Are you content within? Can you embrace the person God made you to be? Nowadays, many individuals resort to plastic surgery and alter their appearances. Does this imply a lack of self-love? Not necessarily, but it does suggest they are seeking acceptance from others who did not appreciate them as they are. People must accept you in your authentic, unfiltered state in any romantic or platonic relationship.

You can transform into anyone others expect you to be. However, your happiness will be compromised if you don't stay true to yourself. In tough times, when you revert to survival mode, the dynamics of acceptance shift, affecting who will embrace you and what you are willing to do or accept about yourself.

If people like you solely because of the changes you've made to fit in, then when you revert to your true self, they may not accept you. The aim is to identify your lowest self and worst moments, and balance them with your best while letting go of anything that doesn't represent who you truly are.

Let go of expectations, drama, and anything that pressures you into altering your God-given identity to discover your true self. To embrace who we are, we often need to revisit the moments we began to feel the need to change. When did we first believe something was off about us, and why? What led you to pursue that change? While not all change is negative, some changes can have positive effects.

Certain factors can negatively impact our authentic selves. Love changes your entire mindset. It affects what you are willing to accept, determines what you are ready to offer, reshapes your willingness to venture out, and redefines how you value your essence.

The goal here is soul, purpose, and growth. You will completely shift your perspective by identifying your purpose and nurturing growth through self-love, acceptance, recognizing your gifts, and understanding your calling. This clarity will affect how you engage with your long-term calling and alter your view of others. Ultimately, love is the essential key to transforming your life experience.

Part 2: Prioritize Self-Care

What commitment are you ready to make to love yourself more? How can you enhance your self-love? Is there something about yourself that you've been denying and need to accept? Often, we find ourselves in denial about small things. However, I want to emphasize that you should not compare yourself to others. Just as they may be seen as beautiful, intelligent, and attractive, someone views you as beautiful, intelligent, and attractive, too.

Everyone possesses unique differences, talents, skills, gifts, and abilities. Each person has a distinct background. Even two children raised in the same household can view their upbringing differently, interpreting their experiences, observations, actions, and learnings from that environment in various ways.

Once you achieve self-love, the goal is to learn to love not only yourself but also those you attract. Ultimately, the aim is to embody love, becoming a living testament to its essence, serving as a pillar and an example of love for those around you. This journey starts with improving the way you communicate. That does not mean you don't cuss or get frustrated. Love still experiences emotions, and we all have different emotions.

Love centers around a single aspect that brings you happiness, regardless of your circumstances or emotions. It involves recognizing what truly brings joy to your heart and life. The ultimate aim of spiritual human behavior is to create a life defined by love, to grasp your purpose, and to embark on your mission. This journey entails achieving your life goals and discovering what brings you joy, peace, and love. This understanding enhances your ability to love yourself. Therefore, treat yourself to a date and take time to pray.

You don't need to attend church or identify as religious to pray. Meditating, praying, and connecting with your concept of God, the creator, or any higher power that guides your life is beneficial. Request guidance, seek clarity, and ask for the removal of toxic individuals and influences. Eliminate anything unhelpful that hinders your ability to love yourself, your children, or grow. Understanding yourself is crucial to self-love, and self-acceptance is essential for internal and external love.

You must understand there will be hold-ups; things will come into your life that make you question, like a paradox, whether you're on the right path. The only way to determine this is by sensing how your inner peace aligns with the love within and the connections to those meant to accompany you. The love intended to foster your growth can also provide peace during moments of correction. This love resonates with your journey, reflecting what you are willing to accept about yourself, which is also essential for accepting others.

Your love for yourself activates the love you resonate with in those meant to be in your life and those who do not bring peace. You let go of toxic people because you resonate with love, peace, and joy, drawing in those who bring these qualities even in challenging times. That's how you discern who is who, as they will offer peace even when challenges persist.

If you love yourself and desire others to experience that same love, as you navigate your challenges and healing, you'll realize that the person you're judging also needs healing. The individual you mock may have been hurt just as you were. You cannot know the experiences that shape their thoughts and feelings, just as they may not understand your journey or why you think and act as you do. However, once you start to grasp the concept of love, you will begin to comprehend the world around you. This is why having faith is valuable.

Hope is beneficial, but love surpasses it. When you genuinely love yourself, you can love others effectively. It's essential to recognize that activating your love helps balance your inner self. This alignment naturally attracts others who resonate with your vibe, understanding who you are and who they are meant to be on this shared journey.

The essential factor is recognizing your identity, desires, and aspirations. This self-awareness allows you to effortlessly identify individuals who are meant to be in your life, helping you avoid unfavorable situations while determining their compatibility with you. It is also crucial to grasp what God is currently doing in your life during this season. As you gain insight into God's workings, you will clarify who should be part of your journey.

Connecting with yourself enables authentic connections with others who resonate with you; together, you'll share a journey where mutual love is recognized. This inner love will attract your soulmate or twin flame, embodying the long-lasting love that many of us long for and desire.

Thank you for your purchase. You can also follow us online on IG and FanBase @SpeakingFreedom, You can find our YouTube Channel yourtube.com/@speakingfreedomTV

Please check out our other books.

Faith 101

Faith 201

Faith 301

Faith 401

The Unknown Power

It's My Time

www.ingramcontent.com/pod-product-compliance
Lightning Source LLC
Chambersburg PA
CBHW070045080526
44586CB00013B/925